PARABLES OF THE MESSIAH

Activity Book

Parables of the Messiah Activity Book

Bible Pathway Adventures® is a trademark of BPA Publishing Ltd.

ISBN: 978-1-98-858569-7

Author: Pip Reid

Creative Director: Curtis Reid

For free Bible resources including coloring pages, worksheets, puzzles and more, visit our website at:

www.biblepathwayadventures.com

◇ INTRODUCTION ◇

Enjoy teaching your students about the Bible with our *Parables of the Messiah activity book*. Packed with Bible passages, puzzles, and fun worksheets – all designed to help children learn about the Messiah in a fun and engaging way. Includes scripture references for easy Bible verse look-up, and an answer key for educators. The perfect resource for Sabbath and Sunday School classes, and homeschooling.

Bible Pathway Adventures helps educators teach children the Biblical faith in a fun and creative way. We do this via our illustrated storybooks, Teacher Packs, and printable activities – all available on our website: www.biblepathwayadventures.com

Thanks for buying this Activity Book and supporting our ministry. Every book purchased helps us continue our work providing free Classroom Packs and discipleship resources to families and missions around the world.

The search for Truth is more fun than Tradition!

◆◇ TABLE OF CONTENTS ◇◆

◇◇ TAKE A TRIP BACK IN TIME ◇◇

Our vision is to provide culturally, historically, and biblically sound materials to help you teach your children a Biblical faith. When we read the Bible in the context of the ancient Hebrew culture, it comes alive and unlocks the beauty and richness of the faith.

Why do we use Hebrew names like Yeshua? Or sometimes include the Hebrew names for God like Yah? Because understanding these ancient names and cultures helps us unlock the richness of each Biblical account – a richness and understanding that can get lost, changed, or watered-down when only seen from a modern Western perspective.

For example, Matthew 26:34 says… "Before the rooster crows, you will deny me three times." In its cultural and historical context, this was not actually a rooster crowing but the Temple Crier, a priest who announced the morning Temple services and sacrifices at the time of Yeshua. Did you know the modern English name of 'Jesus' has only been used for 500 years? This means Mary and the disciples would have called the Messiah by His actual Hebrew name, Yeshua or Yehoshua, which means, 'God saves,' or 'God is my salvation.' Isn't that wonderful!

So…let's take a trip back in time and enjoy the richness of the Bible!

THE LOST SHEEP

Read Matthew 18:12-14. Fill in the blanks below.

" What do you think? If a man has a ....*Hundred*.......... sheep and one of them has gone ....*astray*.........., does he not leave the ninety-nine on the ....*mountains*.......... and go in search of the one that went astray? And if he finds it, truly, I say to you, he ....*Rejoices*.......... over it more than over the ....*Ninety-nine*.......... that never went astray. So it is not the will of My ....*father*.......... who is in ....*Heaven*.......... that one of these little ones should ....*Perish*.......... . "

HUNDRED	FATHER
MOUNTAINS	ASTRAY
REJOICES	PERISH
NINETY-NINE	HEAVEN

THE LOST SHEEP

Read Matthew 18:10-14.
Answer the questions below.

1. Who do the angels see the face of in heaven?

2. How many sheep does a man have?

3. Where does he leave the ninety-nine sheep?

4. What does the man do when he finds the missing sheep?

5. Where is the Father?

6. What is the Father's Will?

7. Who spoke this parable?

Jehovah

one Hundred

on a mountain

Rejoices

in heaven

that none perish

Jesus

THE LOST SHEEP

Read Matthew 18:10-14.
Find and circle each of the words from the list below.

WILL   SHEEP   ASTRAY   FATHER
ONE HUNDRED   ANGELS   MAN   MOUNTAINS
PERISH   REJOICE   HEAVEN   SHEPHERD

11/20

The Lost Sheep

Draw a picture a shepherd with his sheep.

If the parable of the lost sheep was a book, the cover would look like this...

This parable teaches me…

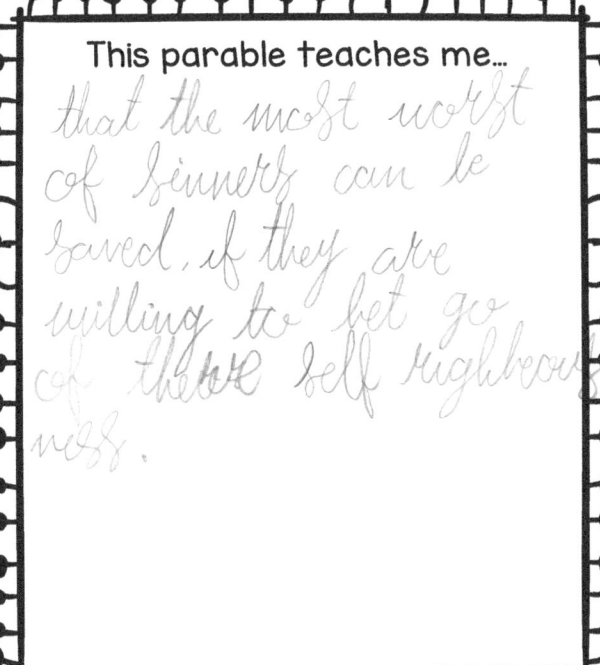

that the most worst of sinners can be saved. if they are willing to let go of there self righteousness.

Write a poem about the parable of the lost sheep.

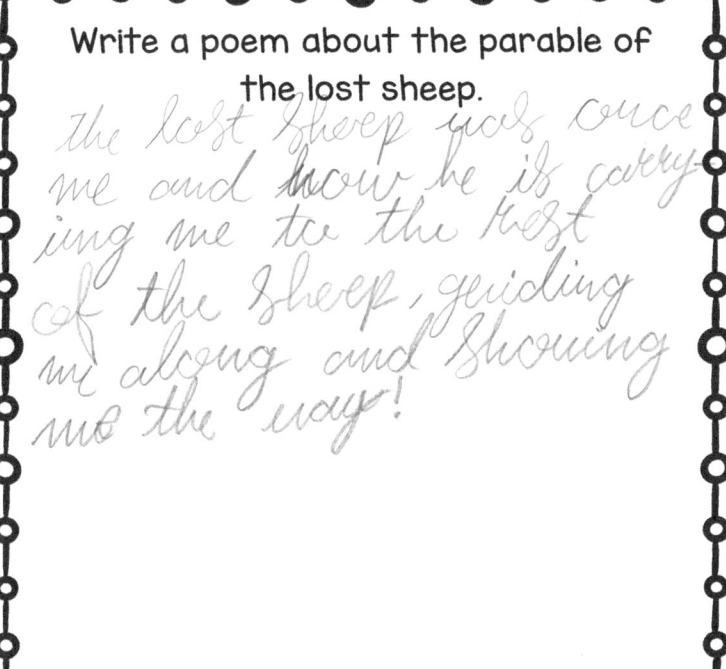

the lost sheep was once me and now he is carrying me to the rest of the sheep, guiding me along and showing me the way!

THE LOST SHEEP

Open your Bibles and read Matthew 18:12-14.
Answer the questions. Color the picture.

1. How many sheep did the man have? (verse 12)

....

....

....

....

2. How many sheep went missing? (verse 12)

....

....

....

....

3. What did the man do when He found the missing sheep? (verse 13)

....

....

....

....

CRACK THE CODE!

The Bible verse is written in code. Use the alphabet chart at the bottom of the page to fill in the missing letters and crack the code! *Hint: Read Matthew 18:14 (ESV)*

```
__  __   I   I   __ __  __ __ __ __  __ __  I  __ __  __ F  __ __
12  2   10  15  10 12  9  2  15 15 26 3  24 10 6  6   2  16 18 1
```

```
 F  A  __ __ __ __ __ __ __    I  __   I  __ __ __  A  __ __ __ __ __  A  __
16 25 15 26 3 23 24 26 2   10 12  10  9 26 3 25  5  3  9  15 26 25 15
```

```
__ __ __  __ F  __ __ __ __ __ __   __  I  __ __ __ __  __ __ __ __
 2  9  3   2 16 15 26 3 12 3   6  10 15 15 6  3   2  9  3 12
```

```
__ __ __ __ __ __  __ __ __  I  __ __
12 26 2  8  6 20  11  3 23 10 12 26
```

A	B	C	D	E	F	G	H	I	J	K	L	M
25					16			10				

N	O	P	Q	R	S	T	U	V	W	X	Y	Z

Let's Write

Read the parable of the Lost Sheep.
Write the story in your own words on the lines below.

My Bible notes

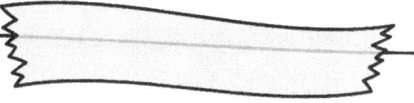

Draw your favorite scene from this parable.

Use this space to write what God showed me today:

_____

_____

_____

_____

_____

WORKERS IN THE VINEYARD

Read Matthew 20:1-16. Fill in the blanks below.

66 The kingdom of .... is like a master of a house who hired workers for his vineyard early one morning. He agreed with the workers for a denarius a day and sent them to his vineyard. Going out about the third hour he saw others doing nothing in the marketplace and said to them, 'Go to the .... and whatever is right I will give you.' Going out again about the sixth hour and the ninth hour, he did the same. About the .... hour he went and found others standing. He said to them, 'Why do you stand here idle all day? 'They said, 'Because no one has hired us.' He replied, 'You go to my vineyard too. 'When evening came, the .... said to his manager, 'Pay the workers their ...., beginning with the last up to the first.' When those hired at the eleventh hour came, each of them received a denarius. When those hired first came, they thought they would receive more but each of them also received a .... They grumbled at the master of the house, saying, 'These last worked only one hour and you have made them .... to us who have worked all day in the heat.' He replied to one of them, 'Friend, I am being fair with you. You agreed to work for a denarius. Take what belongs to you and go. I choose to give to this last worker the same as you. Am I not allowed to do what I choose with what belongs to me? Or do you begrudge my ....? 'So the last will be first and the first last. 99

HEAVEN	DENARIUS
VINEYARD	GENEROSITY
ELEVENTH	WAGES
MASTER	EQUAL

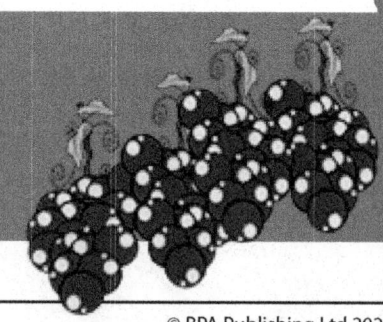

WORKERS IN THE VINEYARD

Read Matthew 20:1-16.
Answer the questions below.

1. What is the kingdom of heaven like? ....

2. What time of the day did the master hire his first group of workers? ....

3. For how much money did the workers agree to work? ....

4. Where did the master send the workers? ....

5. How many more times did the master hire workers? ....

6. Who did the master tell to pay the workers? ....

7. In what order were the workers paid? ....

8. Why did some workers grumble? ....

9. How did the master reply to the grumbling workers? ....

10. "The last will be _____ and the first last." ....

WORKERS IN THE VINEYARD

Read Matthew 20:1-16.
Find and circle each of the words from the list below.

GENEROUS   VINEYARD   LAST   GRUMBLE
HIRE   WORKERS   FIRST   DENARIUS
KINGDOM   HEAVEN   MASTER   WAGES

Workers in the Vineyard

Create a map of the vineyard to give to new workers.

If this parable was a book, the cover would look like this...

This parable teaches me...

Describe the Master's character.

WORKERS IN THE VINEYARD

Open your Bibles and read Matthew 20:1-16.
Answer the questions. Color the picture.

1. For much money did the workers work? (verse 1)

....
....
....
....

2. Who paid the workers their wages? (verse 8)

....
....
....
....

3. "So the last will be _____ and the first last." (verse 16)

....
....
....
....

CRACK THE CODE!

The Bible verse is written in code. Use the alphabet chart at the bottom of the page to fill in the missing letters and crack the code! *Hint: Read Matthew 20:14 (ESV)*

```
_  A  K  E  _  _  A  _  _  E  _  _  _  _  _  _  _  _  _  _  A  _  _
19 5  15 20 17 23 5  19 21 20 10 13 14 7  11 19 13 2  13 3  5  14 18

_  _  .  _  _  _  _  _  _  E  _  _  _  _  _  _  E  _  _  _  _  _
7  13    18 25 23 13 13 11 20 19 13 7  18 22 20 19 13 19 23 18 11

_  A  _  _  _  _  _  K  E  _  A  _  _  _  _  _  _  E  _  _  _  _
10 5  11 19 17 13 16 15 20 16 5  11 18 7  18 22 20 19 13 2  13 3
```

A	B	C	D	E	F	G	H	I	J	K	L	M
5				20						15		

N	O	P	Q	R	S	T	U	V	W	X	Y	Z

★ Let's Write ★

Read the parable of the Workers in the Vineyard.
Write the story in your own words on the lines below.

⭐ My Bible notes ⭐

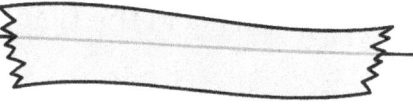

Draw your favorite scene from this parable.

Use this space to write what God showed me today:

_____

_____

_____

_____

_____

THE MUSTARD SEED

Read Mark 4:30-34. Fill in the blanks below.

" He said, "With what can we compare the .... of God, or what

.... shall we use for it? It is like a grain of ....

seed, which when sown on the ground is the smallest of all the .... on

earth. Yet when it is sown, it .... up and becomes larger than all the

.... plants and puts out large branches, so that the

.... of the air can make nests in its shade." With many such parables

He spoke the word to them, as they were able to hear it. He did not speak to them without a

parable. But privately to His own ...., Yeshua explained everything. "

KINGDOM   BIRDS
PARABLE   DISCIPLES
MUSTARD   GARDEN
GROWS   SEEDS

THE MUSTARD SEED

Read Mark 4:30-34.
Answer the questions below.

1. With what does Yeshua compare the kingdom of heaven? ....

2. How small is the mustard seed when sown? ....

3. How big does the mustard seed become when it grows up? ....

4. What are the birds of the air able to do? ....

5. What did Yeshua always include when He spoke with the people? ....

6. What did Yeshua say privately to His disciples? ....

7. Who spoke this parable? ....

THE MUSTARD SEED

Read Mark 4:30-34.
Find and circle each of the words from the list below.

```
H C Q U E L C J K V R K Q R K K B J U M
A H S D I S C I P L E S Y T H X F A B Q
X N H Z V A Z B C T U M S X Z C C X I X
Z T K M B V X V R Y D F Z X A C A I R Q
C Z Z N U Q F G U A B H U K L N R N D W
Y Q Y W Q S U N C U N G D C O N A E S T
J L V Z D U T C J I K C O X B K U S K O
N W V U R W T A H L F Z H V P V X T I M
C C O M R P J O R D Z Z P E V S S S N K
X S G V G Q N D F D Y P L R S V Y T G T
W C H I Q A Z O N U I A I B O T G C D P
O N L A I J R W M R Y J K T C K C H O H
B C F L D B Q D W Z P A P Z Y E R R M W
F Z O N Z E Y S E I Z H B W E S W N I W
Z W L Y B X J B Z N A S F B S E I P G E
P Q G G O D S P J H N J K L H E D D D M
E C Q F H B G U D J Z D U M U D A Z E S
L G D P K Y U C D O D S A T A C I Y E Q
N W G J Z P A R A B L E X Q Q Q I D T C
J G K P L G U K X E I V Y V K G P J E P
```

SEED	NESTS	PARABLE	BRANCHES
GOD	SHADE	GARDEN	YESHUA
KINGDOM	MUSTARD	DISCIPLES	BIRDS

The Mustard Seed

Create a diagram to retell the parable of the mustard seed.

If this parable was a book, the cover would look like this...

This parable teaches me...

Disciples are followers of Yeshua. I follow Yeshua by...

A DISCIPLE

Open your Bibles and read Mark 4.
Answer the questions. Color the picture.

1. How many disciples did Yeshua have? (verse 10)

....
....
....
....

2. What did Yeshua speak to the people to explain the Word of God? (verse 34)

....
....
....
....

3. What did Yeshua do when He was alone with His disciples? (verse 34)

....
....
....
....

CRACK THE CODE!

The Bible verse is written in code. Use the alphabet chart at the bottom of the page to fill in the missing letters and crack the code! *Hint: Read Mark 4:31 (ESV)*

I   I   I   I   O   M

7 20   7 15   25 7 16 21 26   24 11 26 7 9   19 23   4 2 15 20 26 11 8

              I   O   O

15 21 21 8 , 22 18 7 5 18 , 22 18 21 9 15 19 22 9 19 9 20 18 21

       O   I   M   O

24 11 19 2 9 8 , 7 15 20 18 21 15 4 26 25 25 21 15 20 19 23

                            O

26 25 25 20 18 21 15 21 21 8 15 19 9 21 26 11 20 18

A	B	C	D	E	F	G	H	I	J	K	L	M
								7				4

N	O	P	Q	R	S	T	U	V	W	X	Y	Z
	19											

Let's Write

Read the parable of the Mustard Seed.
Write the story in your own words on the lines below.

★ My Bible notes ★

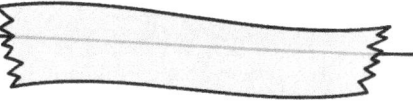

Draw your favorite scene from this parable.

Use this space to write what God showed me today:

_____

_____

_____

_____

_____

THE GOOD SAMARITAN

Read Luke 10:25-37. Fill in the blanks below.

❝ The Torah teacher, desiring to justify himself said to Yeshua, "Who is my...............................?" Yeshua replied, "A man was going down from .... to Jericho and fell among robbers, who stripped him, beat him and departed, leaving him half dead. Now by chance a priest was going down that road, and when he saw him he passed by on the other side. Likewise, a .... when he came to the place and saw him, passed by on the other side. But a Samaritan, as he journeyed, came to where he was and when he saw him, he had .... He bound up his wounds, pouring on oil and wine. Then he set him on his own .... and brought him to an inn and took care of him. The next day he took out two .... and gave them to the innkeeper, saying, 'Take care of him, and whatever more you spend I will repay you when I come back.' Which of these three do you think proved to be a neighbor to the man who fell among the .... ?" He said, "The one who showed him ...." And Yeshua said to him, "Go and do likewise." **❞**

NEIGHBOR   DENARII
JERUSALEM   MERCY
LEVITE   ANIMAL
COMPASSION   ROBBERS

THE GOOD SAMARITAN

Read Luke 10:25-37.
Answer the questions below.

1. Who asked Yeshua how to inherit eternal life? ....

2. How did Yeshua answer this man in Luke 10:27? ....

3. Where was the traveler going in the story? ....

4. What happened to the traveler on this road? ....

5. Who was the first man to walk past? ....

6. Who was the second man to walk past? ....

7. Who was the third man to see the traveler? ....

8. What did the Samaritan do to help the traveler? ....

9. How much did he pay the innkeeper? ....

10. When Yeshua asked the Torah teacher who was the neighbor,

    how did he answer? ....

31

THE GOOD SAMARITAN

Read Luke 10:25-37.
Find and circle each of the words from the list below.

```
M A B P J W X D J W C T S L Z Y L F R U
W C O D F S J W D R L Z D Q R Q T G G U
R E T E O Y U E H I I G G B D S V R A B
O D R N M D Z I R U P E Y M W X R O S W
A S K A W G Q T G I L F P J O S Y B M W
D L L R I J G P R Q C W G Q U Z Q B D C
M Z K I Q E V Q I W A H L T N P B E N T
K Z G I B F X F B X A J O C D R X R N D
G W B O K U J T S P B H L V S I Q S O R
A W H T O R A H T E A C H E R E H W X M
I Q W N O H B C C R L X E O H S D J L C
K Q G F Y I A L P T C P Y U H T O B L V
W I G I W Y X D W S J K W X F Q X F E O
P V O J W P Y N Q N T B U O M J U V V Y
W O F P C F X Q D B D Z Y B F E H U I R
Q N D R C Q X J E R U S A L E M R Y T L
P U M G M T N H H A Y M J V U T Y C E U
F O W T A N I M A L O S P W I N N O Y A
R F U N B B O C S F A X N F K W N X P A
X N Z H V W Y F E P K W P U R R Y F X J
```

ROAD	ROBBERS	JERUSALEM	MERCY
TORAH TEACHER	WOUNDS	ANIMAL	LEVITE
JERICHO	PRIEST	INN	DENARII

Good Samaritan

Draw a picture of the good Samaritan.

If I met someone on the road who had been beaten and robbed, I would…

This parable teaches me…

If the parable of the good Samaritan was a book, the cover would look like this…

THE GOOD SAMARITAN

Open your Bibles and read Luke 10:25-37.
Answer the questions. Color the picture.

1. Which man stopped and helped the traveler?
(verse 33)

....

....

....

....

2. How many denarii did the Samaritan give the innkeeper? (verse 35)

....

....

....

....

3. Who was a neighbor to the man who fell among robbers? (verse 37)

....

....

....

....

 # CRACK THE CODE!

The Bible verse is written in code. Use the alphabet chart at the bottom of the page to fill in the missing letters and crack the code! *Hint: Read Luke 10:33 (ESV)*

B __ __ __ __ __ __ __ __ I __ __ __ , __ __ __ __
10 26 12 16 9 16 2 16 3 8 12 16 1   16 9 25 17

__ O __ __ __ __ Y __ D , __ __ __ __ O __ __ __ __ __ __ __
14 22 26 3 1 17 6 17 4   11 16 2 17 12 22 18 25 17 3 17 25 17

__ __ __ , __ __ D __ __ __ __ __ __ __ __ __ __ I __ , __ __ __ __ D
18 16 9   16 1 4 18 25 17 1 25 17 9 16 18 25 8 2   25 17 25 16 4

__ O __ __ __ __ __ I O __
11 22 2 24 16 9 9 8 22 1

A	B	C	D	E	F	G	H	I	J	K	L	M
	10		4					8				

N	O	P	Q	R	S	T	U	V	W	X	Y	Z
	22										6	

Let's Write

Read the parable of the Good Samaritan.
Write the story in your own words on the lines below.

 # My Bible notes

Draw your favorite scene from this parable.

Use this space to write what God showed me today:

_____

_____

_____

_____

_____

WISE AND FOOLISH VIRGINS

Read Matthew 25:1-13. Fill in the blanks below.

" The kingdom of .... will be like ten virgins who took their lamps and went to meet the .... Five of them were foolish and five were .... When the foolish took their lamps, they took no oil with them. But the wise took flasks of oil with their lamps. As the bridegroom was ...., they all became drowsy and slept. But at .... there was a cry, 'Here is the bridegroom! Come out to meet Him.' Then all the virgins rose and trimmed their .... The foolish virgins said to the wise, 'Give us some of your oil for our lamps are going out.' But the wise virgins said, 'Since there will not be enough for us and for you, go to the dealers and buy for yourselves.' And while they were going to buy, the bridegroom came and those who were ready went in with Him to the .... feast and the door was shut. Afterward the other virgins came, saying, 'Lord, open to us.' But He answered, 'Truly, I say to you, I do not know you.' .... therefore, for you know neither the day nor the hour. "

HEAVEN   LAMPS
BRIDEGROOM   MIDNIGHT
WISE   MARRIAGE
DELAYED   WATCH

WISE AND FOOLISH VIRGINS

Read Matthew 25:1-13.
Answer the questions below.

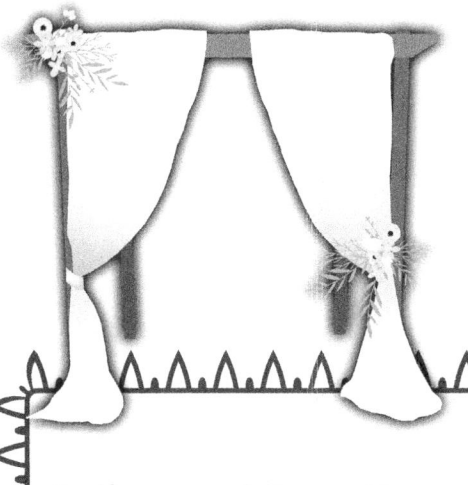

1. How many virgins went to meet the bridegroom? ....

2. How many virgins were wise? ....

3. What happened when the bridegroom was delayed? ....

4. At what time did the virgins hear the bridegroom was

   on His way to meet them? ....

5. What were the virgins told to do? ....

6. What did the wise virgins take with them to meet the bridegroom? ....

7. What did the foolish virgins take with them to meet the bridegroom? ....

8. What did the foolish virgins ask the wise virgins? ....

9. What happened while the foolish virgins went to buy oil? ....

10. Why did the bridegroom not let the foolish virgins into the wedding? ....

WISE AND FOOLISH VIRGINS

Read Matthew 25:1-13.
Find and circle each of the words from the list below.

U K O Y P G Y L R O M K S D F M X S V G
U H Q D Q B I J W B L E Z K P I W C O X
L G B T H K N F N T B L N R Y D E J O W
F M O R W L V M L O M R F Z C N D C M T
L Y C J I V X V B N F J P R D I D K W Z
H N D H G D Q U G Q A N F W J G I L P K
D D T V S M E I X I Z Y Y O Y H N A R R
F Q J I W Z B G Q D A P S V O T G M J A
G Q Q R G Z I M R L Q Q Q W V L W P Z J
G X O G A N H T Z O T U H D T V I S W F
H M S I L W U N O Y O D A O I S M S L M
T E O N T L J X Y Y B M M D K I U R H W
N G A S K I N G D O M F V U G I K B S I
I H D V F Z Y P F R R W Z W P L Z D A S
K U H P E G W R O R O P A T L W N P P E
Q T Z P J N X A H K A W H Q O E A S X I
X X M B R F H Z W Q U Y S U J I M V Y L
Q F H T V T U Q D O S L S Y I E L U H E
B L Q P S E W J G L A C G Y W R C B Y N
F E A S T U U W K Z J J L K Q L V Y B E

WEDDING   LAMPS   VIRGINS   BRIDEGROOM
KINGDOM   WISE   OIL   FOOLISH
FEAST   HEAVEN   MIDNIGHT   DROWSY

Wise and Foolish Virgins

Create a wedding feast for the virgins and bridegroom. Use your imagination!

How would you describe the wise virgins?

This parable teaches me…

If this parable was a book, the cover would look like this…

WISE AND FOOLISH VIRGINS

Open your Bibles and read Matthew 25:1-13.
Answer the questions. Color the picture.

1. How many virgins in this parable? (verse 1)

....
....
....
....

2. How many virgins had oil in their lamps? (verse 4)

....
....
....
....

3. Who went into the marriage feast with the bridegroom? (verse 10)

....
....
....
....

 # CRACK THE CODE!

The Bible verse is written in code. Use the alphabet chart at the bottom of the page to fill in the missing letters and crack the code! *Hint: Read Matthew 25:6-7 (ESV)*

```
 B   A   M                                     A     A
25 24 21  2 21 18  6 11  8  6  4  3 21 21  3 14 12 14 22  2 13  2

       Y  ,                                 B                      M !
 7 12 19     3 14 12 14  6 13 21  3 14 25 12  6 11 14  4 12  1  1 18

    M           M               M  .              A  L  L
 7  1 18 14  1 24 21 21  1 18 14 14 21  3  6 18   21  3 14  8  2 10 10

                                                      A
21  3  1 13 14 17  6 12  4  6  8 13 12  1 13 14  2  8 11

          M M                              L  A  M
21 12  6 18 18 14 11 21  3 14  6 12 10  2 18  5 13
```

A	B	C	D	E	F	G	H	I	J	K	L	M
2	25										10	18

N	O	P	Q	R	S	T	U	V	W	X	Y	Z
											19	

Let's Write

Read the parable of the Wise and Foolish Virgins.
Write the story in your own words on the lines below.

⭐ My Bible notes ⭐

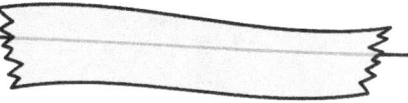

Draw your favorite scene from this parable.

Use this space to write what God showed me today:

_____

_____

_____

_____

_____

THE WEDDING FEAST

Read Matthew 22:1-14. Fill in the blanks below.

" The kingdom of heaven is compared to a king who gave a .... feast for his son and sent servants to call those who were invited to the feast, but they would not come. Again he sent more ...., saying, 'Tell those who are invited, "I have prepared my dinner, my oxen and calves have been killed and everything is ready. Come to the feast."' But they paid no attention and went off, one to his farm, one to his business, while the rest seized his servants, treated them badly and killed them. The king was angry. He sent his .... and destroyed the murderers and burned their city. Then he said to his servants, 'The wedding .... is ready but those invited were not worthy. Go and invite as many as you find.' The servants went and gathered all whom they found, both bad and good. The wedding hall was filled with guests. But when the .... came in to look at the ...., he saw a man who had no wedding garment. He said to him, 'Friend, how did you get in here without a wedding garment?' And he was speechless. The king said to the attendants, 'Bind him hand and foot and cast him into outer .... In that place there will be weeping and gnashing of teeth.' Many are .... but few are chosen. **"**

WEDDING	DARKNESS
SERVANTS	GUESTS
TROOPS	CALLED
FEAST	KING

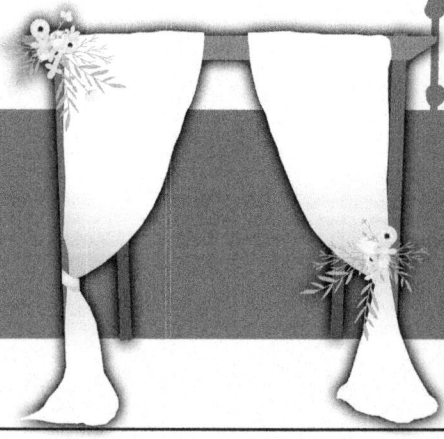

THE WEDDING FEAST

Read Matthew 22:1-14.
Answer the questions below.

1. Who told this parable to the people? ....

2. To whom can the kingdom of heaven be compared? ....

3. For whom did the king hold a wedding feast? ....

4. What animals did the king have slaughtered for the feast? ....

5. What happened to the servants in Matthew 22:6? ....

6. Why did the king destroy the murderers and burn their city? ....

7. Where did the servants gather more wedding guests? ....

8. What did the king see at the feast? ....

9. What instructions did the king give his servants in Matthew 22:13? ....

10. "For many are _____ but few are chosen." (Mat 22:14) ....

THE WEDDING FEAST

Read Matthew 22:1-14.
Find and circle each of the words from the list below.

```
G Q U V I   G E R S X L K C G Y M X G Z C
Q B H Z F Q K Y F E E N I F V A K Z P F
O F S D T A L Y S G R K D G W E B R T E
H R T C X W R Q M Z A V K T M W X T W A
L I L F Z U A C H Y C R A K L Z Y E H S
B M Z L O K P E W F K Q M N F G X P D T
H O C C D S M C Y I J T T E T C H P U I
D J A L T O N W U O J C R H N S T S H N
L N L W E D D I N G A W A Q L T A Y S Z
W G V N F J R B M A V V I Z R X S R P R
G U E F V S P Y Q V I Y V H T K I N G O
L M D L A U U E R O P A Y J H P A Z J J
Q D D S W R Y M N M W Z P N R G Z V O V
P N G F F E M G S Y V F J O Z F K Q J K
O A G Q A Z B D Y I O T W J M E L O L W
B W C E M H B Q E O E B G J H I L B J C
J X P U C H O S E N M H L W K A T V W R
T G O X E N Q P E B I K U R S X L A L O
G U E S T S Y Q K A Y H Y Y A N T L C E
Q V R O A D S X B Z V F H C Z K R K K Z
```

HALL	GARMENTS	KING	CALVES
CHOSEN	SERVANTS	FARM	GUESTS
FEAST	ROADS	OXEN	WEDDING

The Wedding Feast

Draw a picture of the wedding feast.

Write a description of the wedding feast.

This parable teaches me…

Design a wedding invitation to give to your friends.

THE WEDDING FEAST

Open your Bibles and read Matthew 22:1-14.
Answer the questions. Color the picture.

1. Who did the king send to gather the wedding guests? (verse 3)

....

....

....

....

2. What happened to the king's servants? (verse 6)

....

....

....

....

3. Where did some servants go to find more wedding guests? (verses 9-10)

....

....

....

....

 # CRACK THE CODE!

The Bible verse is written in code. Use the alphabet chart at the bottom of the page to fill in the missing letters and crack the code! *Hint: Read Matthew 22:2 (ESV)*

```
_  _  E    _  _  _  G  _  _  _    _  _    _  E  _  _  E  _  _  _  _
18 26 8    9 19 20 1 13 15 23   15  4    26 8  5  6  8 20 23  5 17

B  E    _  _  _  _  _  E  _  _  _    _    _  _  _  G    _  _  _
16 8    21 15 23 12 5 24 8 13 18 15  5    9 19 20 1    14 26 15

G  _  _  E  _    _  E  _  _  _  _  G    _  E  _  _  _  _  _  _
1  5  6  8  5    14 8 13 13 19 20 1    4  8  5  3 18  4 15 24

                      _  _  _    _  _  _
                      26 19 3    3 15 20
```

A	B	C	D	E	F	G	H	I	J	K	L	M
	16			8		1					22	

N	O	P	Q	R	S	T	U	V	W	X	Y	Z

Let's Write

Read the parable of the Wedding Feast.
Write the story in your own words on the lines below.

★ My Bible notes ★

Draw your favorite scene from this parable.

Use this space to write what God showed me today:

_____

_____

_____

_____

_____

THE PRODIGAL SON

Read Luke 15:11-32. Fill in the blanks below.

" A man had two sons. The younger son said to his father, 'Give me my share of the inheritance.' The man divided his wealth between them. A few days later, the .... son gathered all he had, went to a far land and wasted his inheritance on foolish living. When he had spent everything, there was a .... and he became hungry. He got a job with a man who sent him into his fields to feed pigs. He was so hungry that he wanted the food that the .... ate. But no one gave him anything. He said, 'My father's hired workers have plenty of food. I have nothing to eat. I will return home and say to my father, "I have sinned against .... and before you. I am no longer worthy to be called your son. Treat me as one of your hired workers."' He left and went to his father. While he was still a long way off, his father saw him coming. He felt compassion and ran to him, and hugged and kissed him. The son said, 'I have sinned against heaven and before you. I am not worthy to be called your son.' The father said to his workers, 'Put the best robe on him, put a ring on his hand and shoes on his feet. Kill the best .... and let us eat and celebrate. My son was dead, and is alive again; he was lost and now is found.' So they began to celebrate. The .... son was in the field and as he came near the house, he heard music and dancing. He asked a .... what was happening. He said, 'You father has killed the best calf because your brother is back home safely.' But the son was angry and refused to go in. His father came out and pleaded with him, but he said, 'I have served you for many years and never .... you. You never gave me a young goat to celebrate with my friends. But my brother comes home who has used his inheritance with prostitutes and you killed the best calf for him!' He said to him, 'Son, you are always with me and everything I have is yours. It was fitting to celebrate and be happy - your brother was dead and is alive; he was lost and is found.' "

YOUNGER	CALF
FAMINE	SERVANT
PIGS	DISOBEYED
HEAVEN	OLDER

THE PRODIGAL SON

Read Luke 15:11-32.
Answer the questions below.

1. How many sons did the father have? ....

2. Which son asked his father for his inheritance? ....

3. After he left home, where did the son go? ....

4. What happened in the country where the son went? ....

5. After the son wasted his money, what job did he get? ....

6. Why did the son decide to return home? ....

7. Who was not happy about the son's return? ....

8. What did the father do when he saw his youngest son in the distance? ....

9. What did the father give his son when he arrived home? ....

10. What did the father do to celebrate his youngest son's return? ....

THE PRODIGAL SON

Read Luke 15:11-32.
Find and circle each of the words from the list below.

```
F P M P H Z D I O F S H T E I O L L T W
J F I B R U I V X P E C K F T H A P P B
H Z P G G E G Q M N A U O D T D F L H S
O P R D S J T G R E E N L W L K N V P O
V M U B F X K M E L O N D Y F R I B L N
R E R O O W Q M P D F B E F H M F Y E G
M U A S D M T S Q D N H R Q I E Q N L J
D Y G D P U F F L Q J V U M Q O Q Z C A
C S O Y T S Q I Q C P M N S V N X O R G
X L A Y O I J H Y C X H G I S Q H E S M
S Z T N B C B Y P F Q L A D S C A K K J
N M J L I C Z X L J T Z A A P B A K S N
M E F Q G Y Z L S Q R S V N T M T L X A
L G M U O S O F P K I I B M I F J P F E
R R M B B W B U O Q N Z N Y E X L A E A
F K S C C T N X N V G Z X O H K P V Y X
U R G X S Z I G E G K I W E A L T H X K
H H X Q F C P J K R E N Q Y A Q I I H V
E Q R N F A T H E R O R I Y U K Y X Y C
V A H Q C E L E B R A T E U N E C T I A
```

HUGGED	PIGS	FATHER	MUSIC
CELEBRATE	YOUNGER	RING	CALF
OLDER	GOAT	WEALTH	SON

The Prodigal Son

Draw a picture to retell the story of the younger son's life in a faraway land.

If this parable was a book, the cover would look like this...

This parable teaches me...

Imagine you are the older brother. What would you say to your brother when he came home?

THE PRODIGAL SON

Open your Bibles and read Luke 15:11-32.
Answer the questions. Color the picture.

1. What did the father do for his son when he came home? (verses 22-23)

....

....

....

....

2. Why was the father happy to see his son? (verse 27)

....

....

....

....

3. Why did the older son complain to his father? (verse 29)

....

....

....

....

 # CRACK THE CODE!

The Bible verse is written in code. Use the alphabet chart at the bottom of the page to fill in the missing letters and crack the code! *Hint: Read Luke 15:24 (ESV)*

F __ __ T __ __ __ S __ __ __ S __ __ __ __ A S __ __ __ A __ , A __ __
21 23 11   17 24 19 9   13 2 9   23 16 5 15 9   8 10 15 8   15 16 8

__ S A __ __ __ __ A __ A __ __ ; __ __ __ A S __ __ S T
19 9 15 7 19 18 10   15 22 15 19 16   24 10 5 15 9   7 23 9 17

A __ __ S F __ __ __ __ __ . A __ __ T __ __ __ __ __ A __
15 16 8 19 9 21 23 20 16 8   15 16 8   17 24 10 2   25 10 22 15 16

T __ __ __ __ __ __ __ A T __
17 23 3 10 7 10 25 11 15 17 10

A	B	C	D	E	F	G	H	I	J	K	L	M
15					21							

N	O	P	Q	R	S	T	U	V	W	X	Y	Z
					9	17						

Let's Write

Read the parable of the Prodigal Son.
Write the story in your own words on the lines below.

★ My Bible notes ★

Draw your favorite scene from this parable.

Use this space to write what God showed me today:

_____

_____

_____

_____

_____

THE TALENTS

Read Matthew 25:14-30. Fill in the blanks below.

❝ It will be like a man going on a .... who entrusted his servants with his property. To one he gave five talents, to another two, to another one, each according to his ability. Then he went away. He who had received five talents went at once and traded with them, and made five .... more. He who had two talents made two talents more. But he who had received one talent dug in the ground and hid his master's money. After a long time, their master came and settled accounts with them. He who received five talents came forward, bringing five talents more, saying, 'Master, you delivered to me five talents; here, I have made five talents more.' His master said to him, 'Well done, good and faithful .... You have been faithful over a little; I will set you over much. Enter into the joy of your master.' He who had two talents came forward, saying, '..., you delivered to me two talents; here, I have made two talents more.' His master said to him, 'Well done, good and .... servant. You have been faithful over a little; I will set you over much. Enter into the joy of your master.' He who had received the one talent came forward, saying, 'Master, I knew you to be a hard man, ... where you did not sow, and gathering where you scattered no seed, so I was afraid and hid your talent in the ground. Here, you have what is yours.' His master said, 'You .... and slothful servant! You knew that I reap where I have not sown and gather where I scattered no seed? You should have .... my money with the bankers and at my coming I should have received what was mine with interest. Take the talent from him and give it to him who has ten talents. For everyone who has will more be given, and he will have an abundance. But from the one who has not, even what he has will be taken away. Cast the **worthless** servant into the outer darkness where there will be weeping and gnashing of teeth.' ❞

JOURNEY	REAPING
TALENTS	WICKED
SERVANT	MASTER
FAITHFUL	INVESTED

THE TALENTS

Read Matthew 25:14-30.
Answer the questions below.

1. How many talents did the Master give his first servant? ....

2. How many talents did the Master give his second servant? ....

3. How many talents did the third servant receive? ....

4. What did the first servant do with his talents? ....

5. What did the second servant do with his talents? ....

6. What did the third servant do with his talent? ....

7. What did the Master say to his first and second servants when

   he saw them? ....

8. What excuse did the third servant give his Master for doing

   nothing with his talent? ....

9. How did the Master react to the third servant's excuse? ....

10. What did the Master do with that servant's talent? ....

THE TALENTS

Read Matthew 25:14-30.
Find and circle each of the words from the list below.

```
S E E F W N K E I E Y J B Q N W Z M X T
L E W U W B I D X W T O P Y N Z V A P G
G E R M E A J T W L Z P L K X K X S S Q
D Q X V K Q R J U G X K N P M U E T G S
L A D Z A F S K Y Y B N G O E K Q E N J
W B R V U N U X H L W J X J V S F R A R
Q K L K A O T V Q L V Q J O L T A C S D
E P C R N H J S K K E X E S V I I W H Y
V O V T V E L I O P X J O X M N T K I B
H S E E D K S N V X M Z G Q H I H B N L
B Z H T N U W S T A L V S J Y H F M G T
J Q A M L X N K A N I X Q O C D U F B G
J S X V P S O W L J E A G Y E A L Y A K
L X Z S M N I Y E S M G N J R F Z V N Q
I M O N E Y A Q N W Q J T M O F V H K R
I M J M O X U W T Y T S X M E R X K E T
Q M G O K X G M N J J N T E T B H Z R K
V D J M Y B N U K J M T R E A P C Y U F
K Y V X F J B E S R C B Y E C M X N H Z
M S V L L A D Y V B R G L X L K Y N Q R
```

JOY	SERVANTS	SOW	MASTER
TALENT	FAITHFUL	REAP	SEED
DARKNESS	BANKER	MONEY	GNASHING

The Talents

Write a poem about the parable of the talents.

If this parable was a book, the cover would look like this…

This parable teaches me…

If you were suddenly given five talents, what would you do?

PARABLE OF THE TALENTS

Open your Bibles and read Matthew 25:14-30.
Answer the questions. Color the picture.

1. What did the servant who received five talents do with them? (verse 16)

....

....

....

....

2. Why did the servant who received one talent go and bury it? (verse 25)

....

....

....

....

3. Where did Yeshua say to cast the worthless servant? (verse 30)

....

....

....

....

CRACK THE CODE!

The Bible verse is written in code. Use the alphabet chart at the bottom of the page to fill in the missing letters and crack the code! *Hint: Read Matthew 25:21 (ESV)*

```
     M         E                      M,    E
16  6  5 | 12  7  5 23 10  1 |  5  7  6 13 23 17 16  6 12 , | 25 10 18 18

       E ,                     F              F
13 17 20 10 | 24 17 17 13  7 20 13 | 14  7  6 23 16 14 26 18

     E                           E    E E
 5 10  1  4  7 20 23 .  8 17 26 16  7  4 10 11 10 10 20

 F           F              E                       E ;
14  7  6 23 16 14 26 18 | 17  4 10  1  7 | 18  6 23 23 18 10

           E                         E    M    C
 6 25  6 18 18  5 10 23 |  8 17 26 17  4 10  1 | 12 26 19 16
```

A	B	C	D	E	F	G	H	I	J	K	L	M
		19		10	14							12

N	O	P	Q	R	S	T	U	V	W	X	Y	Z

✦ Let's Write ✦

Read the parable of the Talents.
Write the story in your own words on the lines below.

_____

_____

_____

_____

_____

_____

_____

_____

_____

⭐ My Bible notes ⭐

Draw your favorite scene from this parable.

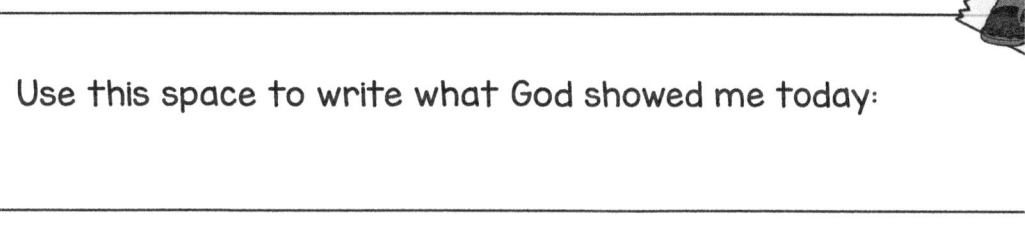

Use this space to write what God showed me today:

_____

_____

_____

_____

_____

THE RICH MAN AND LAZARUS

Read Luke 16:19-31. Fill in the blanks below.

" There was a rich man clothed in .... and fine linen, who feasted every day. At his gate lay a poor man named Lazarus, covered with sores, who desired to be fed with food that fell from the rich man's table. Even the dogs came and licked his sores. The .... man died and was carried by the to Abraham's side. The rich man also died and was buried. In Hades, being in torment, he lifted up his eyes and saw Abraham far off and .... at his side. He called out, 'Father Abraham, have mercy on me and send Lazarus to dip the end of his finger in water and cool my tongue, for I am in anguish in this flame.' But .... said, 'Child, remember that in your .... you received your good things. And Lazarus received bad things; but now he is comforted here and you are in anguish. A great chasm has been fixed between you and us so that those who would pass from here to you may not be able, and none may cross from there to us.' And he said, 'I beg you to send him to my father's house—for I have five brothers—so that he can warn them in case they also come into this place.' But Abraham said, 'They have .... and the Prophets; let them hear them.' And he said, 'No, father Abraham, if someone goes to them from the dead, they will .... ' He said to him, 'If they do not hear Moses and the Prophets, neither will they be convinced if someone should rise from the dead.' "

PURPLE	ABRAHAM
POOR	MOSES
ANGELS	LIFETIME
LAZARUS	REPENT

THE RICH MAN AND LAZARUS

Read Luke 16:19-31.
Answer the questions below.

1. What did the rich man wear?   ....

2. Who lay at his gate?   ....

3. What happened to Lazarus when he died?   ....

4. Where did the rich man go when he died?   ....

5. Who did the rich man see beside Lazarus?   ....

6. What did the rich man ask Abraham? (Luke 16:24)   ....

7. Where did the rich man want Lazarus to go?   ....

8. How many brothers did the rich man have?   ....

9. "They have _____ and the Prophets; let them hear."   ....

10. Why did the rich man think his brothers would repent?   ....

THE RICH MAN AND LAZARUS

Read Luke 16:19-31.
Find and circle each of the words from the list below.

```
D J U T B K W Z R G J E U I Z Q U S A W
F H W L L Z E N B R I N W F K M K X N W
A V Y A R V R J X B D H O G T S Q L G J
T Q K Z R X T D U N E O V M X L V G E O
H G K A G V A R B M V T G W H Z B A L T
E L P R O P H E T S L O G S P O V U S O
R K J U C B B B W D G A L C O Y Y V M N
V A H S E S Y R A K D F K N F C R B V G
E M O S E S L O O J A A F C S E V O V U
R I D M L H Z O T T M P U O D E Y E E E
A K L E U Y B S N B H G M B I O L H J R
W L E F X N Z N W W R E W L E Q U P U F
V G N A B Q Q N L K L P R R D J E U F L
W H J S C N F S H Z S M A S L K H F U A
X W D C U S X T Y P A W T L Z P F L X Y
W V X D F O I O D J M H F E A S T E D W
A V B Q E K I S A B R A H A M T U D T W
M U K S K B R Q S A E D D Q X F S S D K
K W A S T J Y X Q F Q M U L X A K P B P
U K N Q D U O U Y C P K R I C H X D Z Z
```

BROTHERS	PROPHETS	DIED	TONGUE
ABRAHAM	FEASTED	FATHER	MOSES
ANGELS	DOGS	LAZARUS	RICH

Rich Man and Lazarus

Write the names of the first five books of the Bible written by Moses.

How would your life change if you saw someone raised from the dead?

This parable teaches me…

Draw a rich man's banquet. Use your imagination!

THE RICH MAN AND LAZARUS

Open your Bibles and read Luke 16:19-31.
Answer the questions. Color the picture.

1. Who did the rich man see
when he arrived in Hades?
(verse 23)

....

....

....

....

2. What did the rich man ask
Abraham? (verse 24)

....

....

....

....

3. Why did the rich man
want to send Lazarus to his
brothers? (verse 28)

....

....

....

....

CRACK THE CODE!

The Bible verse is written in code. Use the alphabet chart at the bottom of the page to fill in the missing letters and crack the code! *Hint: Read Luke 16:22 (ESV)*

T		P			R		A					A				A	
11	2	15	20	19	19	13	23	12	14	6	4	15	6	12	14	6	3	12	9

	A	R	R					T		A					T	
5	12	13	13	4	15	6	18	26	11	2	15	12	14	7	15	16	9	11	19

A		R	A		A		'					.	T		R				A	
12	18	13	12	2	12	23	9	9	4	6	15	11	2	15	13	4	5	2	23	12	14

A							A				A				R		
12	16	9	19	6	4	15	6	12	14	6	3	12	9	18	1	13	4	15	6

A	B	C	D	E	F	G	H	I	J	K	L	M
12												

N	O	P	Q	R	S	T	U	V	W	X	Y	Z
		20		13		11						

Let's Write

Read the parable of the Rich Man and Lazarus.
Write the story in your own words on the lines below.

My Bible notes

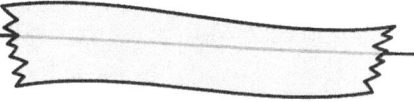

Draw your favorite scene from this parable.

Use this space to write what God showed me today:

_____

_____

_____

_____

_____

❧ THE SOWER ❧

Read Mark 4:1-9. Fill in the blanks below.

" Again Yeshua began to .... beside the sea. A large crowd gathered around Him, so He got into a boat and sat in it on the sea, and the whole crowd was beside the sea on the land. And He was teaching them many things in .... In His teaching, He said to them: "Listen! Behold, a .... went out to sow. And as he sowed, some seed fell along the path and the .... came and ate it. Other seed fell on rocky ground where it did not have much ...., and immediately it sprang up since it had no depth of soil. And when the sun rose, it was .... and since it had no root, it withered away. Other seed fell among thorns, and the thorns grew up and choked it and it grew no grain. And other .... fell into good soil and produced grain, growing up and .... and yielding thirtyfold and sixtyfold and a hundredfold." Yeshua said, "He who has ears to hear, let him hear." **"**

TEACH	SEEDS
PARABLES	SOWER
BIRDS	SOIL
SCORCHED	INCREASING

THE SOWER

Read Mark 4:1-20.
Answer the questions below.

1. Who told this parable to the people?   ....

2. Where did He sit to teach this parable?   ....

3. Where did the crowd gather to hear this parable?   ....

4. What happened to the seeds that fell on the path?   ....

5. What happened to the seeds that fell on rocky ground?   ....

6. What happened to the seeds that fell among thorns?   ....

7. What happened to the seeds that fell into good soil?   ....

8. What did Yeshua say to those around Him with the twelve?   ....

9. What does Satan take away in Mark 4:15?   ....

10. What happens to people who hear the Word and accept it?   ....

THE SOWER

Read Mark 4:1-20.
Find and circle each of the words from the list below.

K Y E Y K C O L N V R C H W O R D E B H
U H F J N A N K V S T T I U T K T U I P
S I H L H E Y R J C N R X M Q U W F R V
E G X B E Y R Q O Z I P Y Z M S A D D W
E Y P Z J V C M V C G S E P T Q X T S U
D Y Y X S O I L D X K X O N A V U M N Z
B X E O G Z S F S M F Y S H N T T K U R
G O B S L V R X T R H Z A K G W T E H W
P F F O H P P O G I V N U K G Q H W V A
N A N U J U C A V H D Y A P U H O V W L
T T R U E V A S B Z G S O W E R R R J N
I Q S A E U V G Y I D G C P R F N A B F
Z J D C B F A M W N P K Y A B D S I G F
M V E L P L J E W R E X T V D L D H U R
T T G T X H E V C E X B C Z N I F B Q U
O L F Z V B R N G M S X S G T P D N O I
Y Y B S P C D Y W C I C B J E L C F I T
R V H C Q P I P H M T C R P O F U L K X
R Y O Q J H O L I A J H K S Q Y P P R R
U E N J K I N G D O M A K L D B N A I J

SEED	SOWER	SOIL	WORD
JOY	ROCKY	FRUIT	YESHUA
KINGDOM	THORNS	PARABLE	BIRDS

The Sower

Draw a diagram to show what happens to the four types of seed.

If this parable was a book, the cover would look like this…

This parable teaches me…

Imagine you were in the crowd listening to this parable. What type of seed are you?

THE SOWER

Open your Bibles and read Mark 4:1-20.
Answer the questions. Color the picture.

1. Where did Yeshua teach this parable? (verse 1)

....

....

....

....

2. What happened to the seeds that fell among the thorns? (verse 7)

....

....

....

....

3. Why happened to the seeds that fell on the good soil? (verse 8)

....

....

....

....

CRACK THE CODE!

The Bible verse is written in code. Use the alphabet chart at the bottom of the page to fill in the missing letters and crack the code! *Hint: Read Mark 4:4 (ESV)*

　　　　　　　 S　H　　　 S
10 26 14　10 4 12 21　4 9 16 21 14 ,　4 9 13 21　4 21 21 14
　　　　　　　　　　　　　　 S　　　　　　 S
　　　　　　　　　　　　 S

　　　　　　　　　　　 T H　　　 T H ,　　　 T H
7 21 20 20 10 20 9 26 1　19 12 21　11 10 19 12 ,　10 26 14　19 12 21

　　　　　 S　　　　　　　　　　　　　 V U　　　　 T
22 8 2 14 4 15 10 13 21 10 26 14　14 21 6 9 5 2 21 14 8 19

A	B	C	D	E	F	G	H	I	J	K	L	M
							12					

N	O	P	Q	R	S	T	U	V	W	X	Y	Z
					4	19	5	6				

✦ Let's Write ✦

Read the parable of the Sower.
Write the story in your own words on the lines below.

★ My Bible notes ★

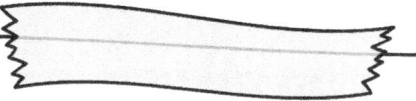

Draw your favorite scene from this parable.

Use this space to write what God showed me today:

_____

_____

_____

_____

_____

THE WISE AND FOOLISH BUILDERS

Read Matthew 7:24-27. Fill in the blanks below.

"Everyone then who hears these .... of Mine and does them will be like a .... man who built his house on the .... The rain fell and the floods came, the .... blew and beat on that house, but it did not fall because it had been founded on the rock. Everyone who hears these words of Mine and does not do them will be like a .... man who built his house on the .... And the rain fell and the .... came, and the winds blew and beat against that ...., and it fell and great was the fall of it. "

WORDS   FOOLISH
WISE   SAND
ROCK   HOUSE
WINDS   FLOODS

THE WISE AND FOOLISH BUILDERS

Read Matthew 7:24-27.
Answer the questions below.

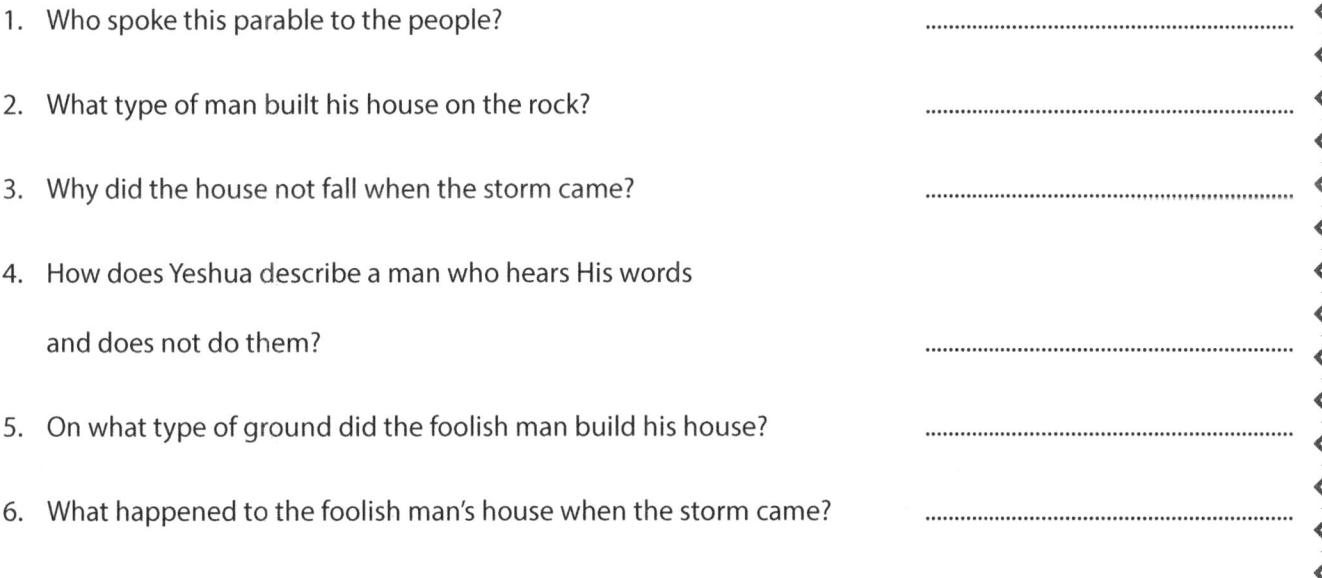

1. Who spoke this parable to the people?

   ....

2. What type of man built his house on the rock?

   ....

3. Why did the house not fall when the storm came?

   ....

4. How does Yeshua describe a man who hears His words

   and does not do them?

   ....

5. On what type of ground did the foolish man build his house?

   ....

6. What happened to the foolish man's house when the storm came?

   ....

THE WISE AND FOOLISH BUILDERS

Read Matthew 7:24-27.
Find and circle each of the words from the list below.

```
X Z H T T S H P Y Q M Y R B L O K T N L
N U Z B D R O P U X N K M P F R U Z F R
N W S U P Y M Z H I G O C W O B O Y H R
P K L I E U T A O U K O J O Z V P C N G
Q Q Q L E Y F M N M S U B A X O W S K A
D Z G D Z M I N X K B U I R E T P P E M
C K F E M W A Y Q M R E T G J R Z E R G
F Q R R O O I C T T D A H O P V H M T P
L X M S D C M N N L H Q I J W J G O H R
G X K E A B V M D J F H D N V M X M P W
D F J Z I N Q R Y Z U H D B I L I N A M
H Q W G Q A D Q Z C O K G X G W Q L Y X
Z O I Q K H D O A H E Z N F S Q F F O X
Q H U C U A B P L S T G W V A J G L P O
Q C W S K G N D J H H Y Q A Q M S B W F
J O E I E R J M B J Y E S H U A V V A E
D I Y X H E F I Y R R V I X O Y I N J L
B N Z W P N G G M W W E C W R A R T S L
E B G K F O O L I S H I W I S E W M L H
V F L O O D D G H J J F N F A Z O E U H
```

WIND	SAND	RAIN	WISE
BUILDER	FLOOD	HOUSE	FOOLISH
ROCK	MAN	FELL	YESHUA

Wise & Foolish Builders

Draw two houses; one build on rock and one built on sand.

It is wise to listen and do what Yeshua says because....

This parable teaches me...

If this parable was a book, the cover would look like this...

 # WISE AND FOOLISH BUILDERS

Open your Bibles and read Matthew 7:24-27.
Answer the questions. Color the picture.

1. Why did the wise man's house not fall down?
(verse 25)

....
....
....
....

2. Why did the foolish man build his house on the sand?
(verse 26)

....
....
....
....

3. What happened to the foolish man's house when the storm came? (verse 27)

....
....
....
....

CRACK THE CODE!

The Bible verse is written in code. Use the alphabet chart at the bottom of the page to fill in the missing letters and crack the code! *Hint: Read Matthew 7:24 (ESV)*

			N		T		N								T			
19	3	19	7	18	8	14	19	25	2	19	14	21	2	8	2	19	6	7	4	25	2	19	4	19

							N			N						T			
21	8	7	17	4	8	13	16	23	14	19	6	14	17	17	8	19	4	25	2	19	16

						K								N			
21	23	9	9	10	19	9	23	11	19	6	21	23	4	19	16	6	14	21	2	8

	U		T						U			N	T					K
10	20	23	9	25	2	23	4	2	8	20	4	19	8	14	25	2	19	7	8	24	11

A	B	C	D	E	F	G	H	I	J	K	L	M
										11		

N	O	P	Q	R	S	T	U	V	W	X	Y	Z
14						25	20					

Let's Write

Read the parable of the Wise and Foolish Builders.
Write the story in your own words on the lines below.

My Bible notes

Draw your favorite scene from this parable.

Use this space to write what God showed me today:

_____

_____

_____

_____

_____

PARABLE OF THE RICH FOOL

Read Luke 12:16-21. Fill in the blanks below.

66 Yeshua told them a .... saying, "The land of a rich man produced many crops and he thought to himself, 'What shall I do - I have nowhere to store my ....?' And he said, 'I will do this: I will tear down my .... and build larger ones, and there I will store all my .... and goods. And I will say to my soul, "Soul, you have many goods laid up for many years; relax, eat, drink, be merry."' But God said to him, '...! This night your .... is required of you and the things you have prepared, whose will they be?' So is the one who lays up .... for himself and is not .... toward God." 99

PARABLE	SOUL
CROPS	TREASURE
GRAIN	BARNS
FOOL	RICH

PARABLE OF THE RICH FOOL

Read Luke 12:16-21.
Answer the questions below.

1. Who told this parable to the people? ....

2. What did the rich man's land produce? ....

3. What did the rich man decide to do with his crops? ....

4. What did he plan to do after he stored his crops? ....

5. What did God say to the rich man? ....

6. What is the meaning of this parable? (Luke 12:21) ....

PARABLE OF THE RICH FOOL

Read Luke 12:16-21.
Find and circle each of the words from the list below.

```
V L S M N I M C R O P S U O C S B W E F
Z Y F I Q N E Y W D G C H W A Y F V A U
G F C E R M R N Y M W R Z Q G H T W T V
X O L X M K R F N S F T S M X R S V I E
C O B E D P Y J Q T R N L Z P Y A M K M
S L Y Z Q U J U O R M M Z M U D W I H X
D J I G N Z F E J E Z J C B Y B E N N I
P F H L Q C Q S R A L W N D P V A I M R
A M B B A D X T M S Y B S V W S P N B Q
K C F Y E S H U A U P G O D X M H S R K
C K Y G T R O B Z R E Q V B H P Y L V H
Q L C U H W Z W Q E Z L T A S G S L X U
P T P G A A N O M D U Z U G W W R D H Q
J N D U T S C B V I A C D R Y F I A D E
G D C Y C U Q G D T H P B B W S C X I X
L A N D L S X Y R I W R G A A W H W A U
U A N A T C U W X N S F X V I R E U Z F
V X M M P M R X H E D Z O R G T N B A R
S O U L K N J P N F R A E Z D M I S S C
D N O P B V O I T M Y P J J X J V X D
```

MERRY	GRAIN	CROPS	FOOL
TREASURE	RICH	BARNS	GOD
LAND	SOUL	EAT	YESHUA

Parable of the Rich Fool

Draw a picture to retell the parable of the rich fool.

Imagine you are a rich man. What would you do if your land produced many crops?

This parable teaches me…

How would you describe the rich man's character?

THE RICH FOOL

Open your Bibles and read Luke 12:16-21.
Answer the questions. Color the picture.

1. Why did the rich man want
to build larger barns?
(verse 17)

....
....
....
....

2. What did the man plan
to put in his bigger barns?
(verse 18)

....
....
....
....

3. What did God say to the
rich man? (verse 20)

....
....
....
....

CRACK THE CODE!

The Bible verse is written in code. Use the alphabet chart at the bottom of the page to fill in the missing letters and crack the code! *Hint: Read Luke 12:20 (ESV)*

Line 1: B(17) _(1) _(18) G(6) _(19) _(25) _(24) _(9) I(10) _(25) _(18) _(19) _(3) _(10) _(5) , _(23) _(19) _(19) _(22) ! _(18) _(3) I(10) _(24)

Line 2: _(14) I(10) G(6) _(3) _(18) _(15) _(19) _(1) _(2) _(24) _(19) _(1) _(22) I(10) _(24) _(2) _(21) _(11) _(1) I(10) _(2) _(21) _(25)

Line 3: _(19) _(23) _(15) _(19) _(1) , _(9) _(14) _(25) _(18) _(3) _(21) _(18) _(3) I(10) _(14) G(6) _(24) _(15) _(19) _(1) _(3) _(9) _(7) _(21)

Line 4: P(12) _(2) _(21) P(12) _(9) _(2) _(21) _(25) , _(26) _(3) _(19) _(24) _(21) _(26) I(10) _(22) _(22) _(8) _(3) _(21) _(15) B(17) _(21) ?

A	B	C	D	E	F	G	H	I	J	K	L	M
	17					6		10				

N	O	P	Q	R	S	T	U	V	W	X	Y	Z
		12										

★ Let's Write ★

Read the parable of the Rich Fool.
Write the story in your own words on the lines below.

My Bible notes

Draw your favorite scene from this parable.

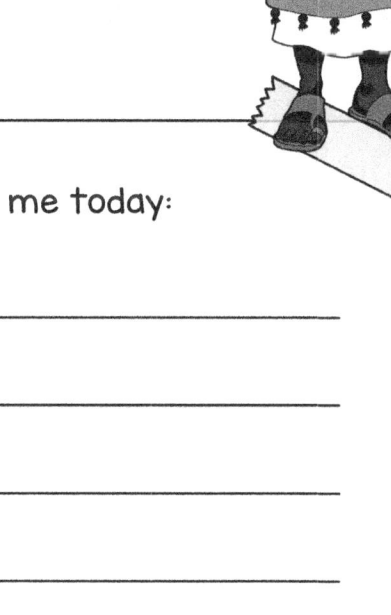

Use this space to write what God showed me today:

_____

_____

_____

_____

_____

THE PHARISEE AND THE TAX COLLECTOR

Read Luke 18:9-14. Fill in the blanks below.

" Yeshua told this parable to some people who thought they were .... and treated others with contempt: "Two men went up into the temple to pray, one a Pharisee and the other a tax collector. The ...., standing alone, prayed, 'God, thank you that I am not like other men who cheat, are unjust, adulterers, or even like this .... collector. I .... twice a week; I give tithes of all that I get.' But the tax collector, standing far off, would not even lift up his eyes to ...., but beat his breast, saying, 'God, have .... on me. I am a ....!' I tell you, this man went down to his house justified rather than the Pharisee. For everyone who exalts himself will be humbled, but the one who .... himself will be exalted. "

RIGHTEOUS	HUMBLES
PHARISEE	SINNER
TAX	FAST
MERCY	HEAVEN

THE PHARISEE AND THE TAX COLLECTOR

Read Luke 18:9-14.
Answer the questions below.

1. Who told this parable to the people? ....

2. Which two men went up to the temple? ....

3. Why did these two men go up to the temple? ....

4. How many times a week did the Pharisee fast? ....

5. In which direction could the tax collector not look? ....

6. What did the tax collector say to God? ....

7. How did the tax collector go down to his house? ....

8. "Everyone who exalts himself will be _____ but the one who

   humbles himself will be exalted." ....

www.biblepathwayadventures.com
Parables of the Messiah Activity Book
103

THE PHARISEE AND THE TAX COLLECTOR

Read Luke 18:9-14.
Find and circle each of the words from the list below.

```
H O U S E Y N N D J Y U Y B V N K F P Z
R O Q F M X Z V Q G W A G M B E B G Z J
C U T X H P K Q V B P E H X P X Q O I Z
R L M A Y B I T E H R O H P J A Q J G O
N R B N X H S I Y B A B L Y P L R R S F
U C O V H C N O I G Y K F A V T A H P K
X B M F Q N O I M Y R H B L S H D X D G
H Q D F Q X P L L I H O V M V U Z M V Z
T E B X W A Q I L A T I V E C M G Y N G
E P A N Q P V X C E S K J R A B E X I P
E H J V Z X E J Q O C Z A C Z L W T D A
Q A M U E G K R Y Y O T Q Y H E P V F R
J R M W C N F U X U P M O L G D L W O A
C I L L V Y F J X H B R D R P L L L I B
K S C D J I H E W J F P J T A A D E D L
T E M P L E V I K A S X H U F R Y Z Y E
V E N Z F X O I M G H O M G P T A E H E
T X G Q K F N P K A G S I N N E R W B E
V J Q T F X R I G H T E O U S S B R Q X
V N Q Q R Q V Z O M B Q F Z V R S S K Y
```

RIGHTEOUS   SINNER   HUMBLED   TAX COLLECTOR
EXALT   PRAY   HEAVEN   PHARISEE
TEMPLE   HOUSE   PARABLE   MERCY

www.biblepathwayadventures.com
Parables of the Messiah Activity Book
104

The Pharisee & the Tax Collector

If this parable was an app, the avatar would look like this...

Research and draw a simple diagram of the temple at the time of Yeshua.

This parable teaches me...

Finish this sentence: Everyone who exalts himself...

THE PHARISEE

Open your Bibles and read Luke 18:9-14.
Answer the questions. Color the picture.

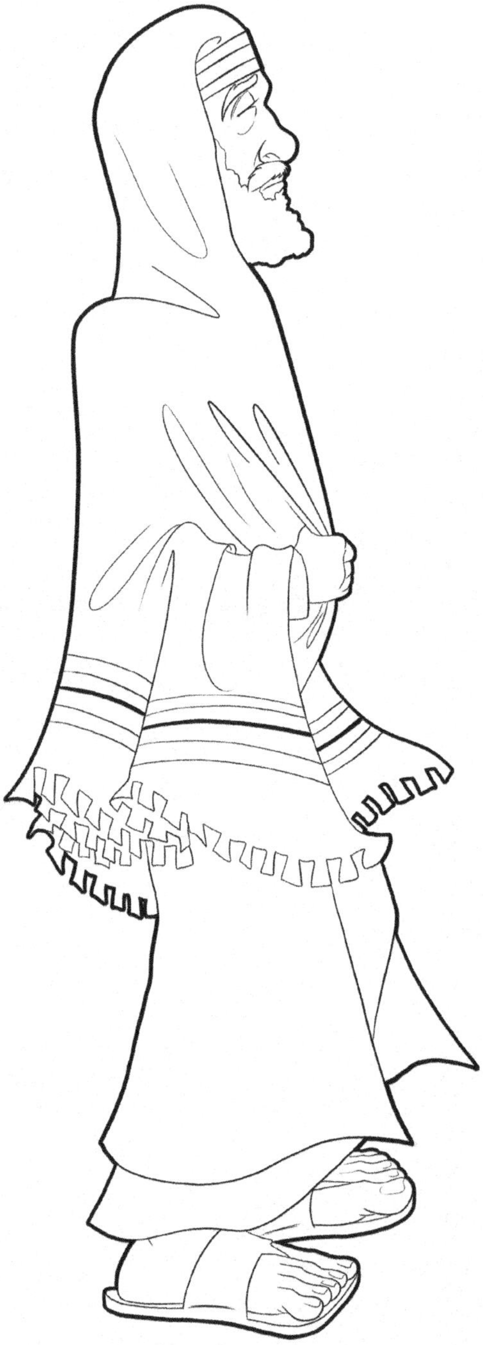

1. To whom did Yeshua tell this parable? (verse 9)

....

....

....

....

2. Who went to the temple to pray? (verse 10)

....

....

....

....

3. Why did the Pharisee think he was better than the tax collector? (verse 12)

....

....

....

....

 # CRACK THE CODE!

The Bible verse is written in code. Use the alphabet chart at the bottom of the page to fill in the missing letters and crack the code! *Hint: Read Luke 18:14 (ESV)*

F O _ _ _ _ _ O _ H O _ _ L _ _ _ _
3 17 23 12 5 12 23 24 17 19 12 26 2 17 12 21 15 7 20 1

H _ _ _ _ _ F _ L L _ _ H _ _ L _ _ , _ _ _
2 8 14 1 12 7 3 26 8 7 7 18 12 2 16 14 18 7 12 25 18 16 20

_ H _ O _ _ H O H _ _ L _ _ H _ _ _ L F
20 2 12 17 19 12 26 2 17 2 16 14 18 7 12 1 2 8 14 1 12 7 3

_ _ L L _ _ _ _ L _ _ _
26 8 7 7 18 12 12 21 15 7 20 12 25

A	B	C	D	E	F	G	H	I	J	K	L	M
					3		2				7	

N	O	P	Q	R	S	T	U	V	W	X	Y	Z
	17											

www.biblepathwayadventures.com
Parables of the Messiah Activity Book

© BPA Publishing Ltd 2020

Let's Write

Read the parable of the Pharisee and the Tax Collector.
Write the story in your own words on the lines below.

My Bible notes

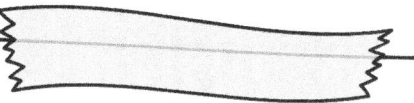

Draw your favorite scene from this parable.

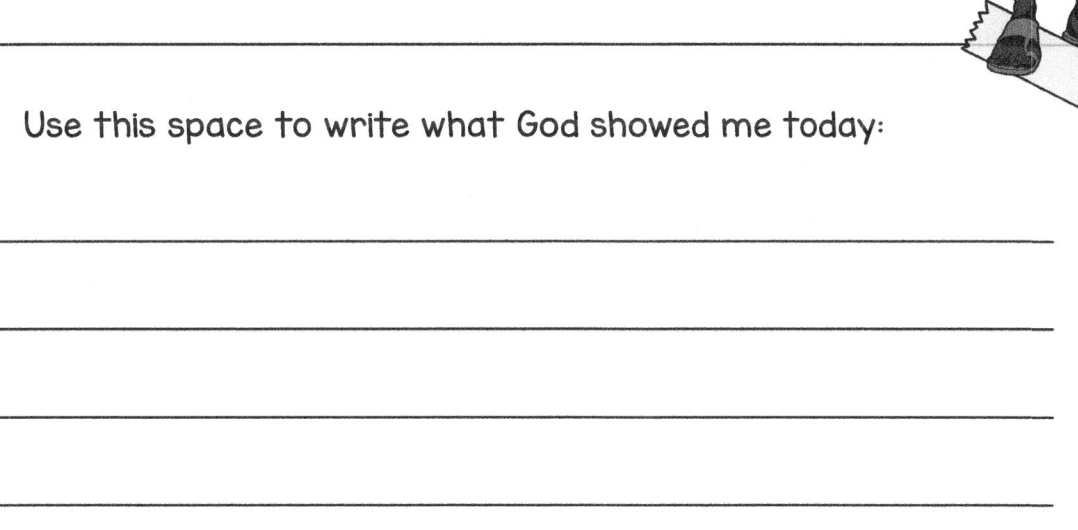

Use this space to write what God showed me today:

_____

_____

_____

_____

_____

THE FAITHFUL SERVANT

Read Luke 12:41-48. Fill in the blanks below.

> Peter said, "Yeshua, are you telling this parable for us or for all people?" Yeshua said, "Who then is the .... and wise .... whom his master will set over his household to give them their portion of .... at the proper time? Blessed is that servant whom his master will find doing so when he comes. Truly, I say to you, he will set him over all his .... But if that .... says to himself, 'My master is delayed in coming,' and begins to beat other servants, and to eat and drink and get drunk, the master of that servant will come on a day when the servant is not ready and not expecting him, and will cut him in pieces and put him with the .... That servant who knew his master's will but did not get ready or do what the .... wanted, will receive a severe beating. But the one who did not know, and did what deserved a beating, will receive a light .... To whoever much was given, much will be required. And much more will be expected from the one who has been given more."

FAITHFUL	BEATING
FOOD	POSSESSIONS
SERVANT	MANAGER
MASTER	UNFAITHFUL

THE FAITHFUL SERVANT

Read Luke 12:41-48.
Answer the questions below.

1. Who spoke this parable to the people? ....

2. Which disciple is mentioned in this parable? ....

3. Who did the master set over his household? ....

4. Who will be blessed when the master comes? ....

5. What will be the faithful servant's reward? ....

6. What will happen to the servant who thought the master

   was delayed, and behaved badly? ....

7. Who will receive a severe beating? ....

8. What will happen to the servant who did not know the

   master's will and did what deserved a beating? ....

9. "To whom ____ was given, much will be required." ....

THE FAITHFUL SERVANT

Read Luke 12:41-48.
Find and circle each of the words from the list below.

```
A W G Z F A I T H F U L C K Z I B N T J
X B M A S T E R C Q I Y D Z Q B D E V F
B X H L G Q A I U N C S Z U M B O U G L
J D D S K X O T P B C F Z H A B D A U T
L I S P U X R Y D P H F P X W F I G N Q
B D H X I W E N J M F V B C P T B R F F
T W R O L T Z P A D P A G Y E S H U A R
M R R F U L O Y K I Q P Y H O C A R I Y
P M N O R S Z B S V L Z N Y H U Y J T B
H R I Q L R E C M R D Y T A K Z F O H B
E R D V Z O R H S Q W X P W T F S J F E
P S J R U L K F O A P M F T N E V M U A
E O Z J I F C F K L R T N A I O Q D L T
T W S O P N X U I A D N A J D X Z X H I
E I K L K P K B I W R W U N E D Z E C N
R S P O J G Z O O K H M Y P L S L C E G
A E J D M Z A X U B Y F F Z A K L F J R
P O S S E S S I O N S M Z Z Y T R R G T
H J L P O P F O O D U I L Y X C N J W M
W Z F E N M C N Q M Q R Z I K U H R H X
```

PETER   FAITHFUL   HOUSEHOLD   MASTER
BEATING   POSSESSIONS   UNFAITHFUL   DELAY
DRINK   WISE   FOOD   YESHUA

www.biblepathwayadventures.com
Parables of the Messiah Activity Book
112

The Faithful Servant

Design a house for the faithful
servant to manage.
Use your imagination!

If this parable was a book, the
cover would look like this…

This parable teaches me…

Imagine you are the Master. What
would you say to your unfaithful
servant when you came home?

THE FAITHFUL SERVANT

Open your Bibles and read Luke 12:41-48.
Answer the questions. Color the picture.

1. What is the faithful and
wise manager's job?
(verse 42)

....
....
....
....

2. What will be the faithful
and wise manager's reward?
(verse 44)

....
....
....
....

3. "To whom much is _____,
much will be required."
(verse 48)

....
....
....
....

 # CRACK THE CODE!

The Bible verse is written in code. Use the alphabet chart at the bottom of the page to fill in the missing letters and crack the code! *Hint: Read Luke 12:43 (ESV)*

B __ __ __ __ __ __ __ __   T __ T __   __ R __ __ __ T   __ O __
22 3 8 10 10 8 2 26 10   17 15 18 17   10 8 6 11 18 16 17   5 15 4 12

__ __ __   __ __ __ T __ R   __ __ __ __   __ __ __ __   __ O   __ O __ __ __
15 26 10   12 18 10 17 8 6   5 26 3 3   19 26 16 2   10 4   2 4 26 16 25

__ __ __ __   __ __   C O __ __ __
5 15 8 16   15 8   7 4 12 8 10

A	B	C	D	E	F	G	H	I	J	K	L	M
	22	7										

N	O	P	Q	R	S	T	U	V	W	X	Y	Z
	4			6		17						

www.biblepathwayadventures.com
Parables of the Messiah Activity Book
115

Let's Write

Read the parable of the Faithful Servant.
Write the story in your own words on the lines below.

_____

_____

_____

_____

_____

_____

_____

_____

www.biblepathwayadventures.com
Parables of the Messiah Activity Book
116

My Bible notes

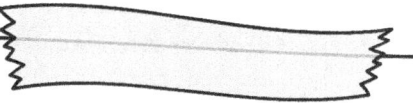

Draw your favorite scene from this parable.

Use this space to write what God showed me today:

_____

_____

_____

_____

_____

THE TWO DEBTORS

Read Luke 7:40-50. Fill in the blanks below.

" Yeshua said to Simon, "I have something to say to you." And he answered, "Say it, Teacher."

"A certain .... had two debtors. One owed 500 .... and the other 50 denarii. When they could not pay, he cancelled the debt of both. Which of them will love him more?" .... answered, "The one, I suppose, for whom he cancelled the larger debt." Yeshua said to him, "You have judged rightly." Then He turned toward the .... and said to Simon, "Do you see this woman? I entered your house; you gave Me no water for My feet, but she has wet My feet with her tears and wiped them with her hair. You gave Me no ...., but from the time I came in she has not ceased to kiss My feet. You did not anoint My head with oil, but she has anointed My feet with .... I tell you, her many sins are forgiven—for she loved much. But he who is forgiven little, loves little." And He said to her, "Your sins are forgiven." Then those who were at table with Him began talking to each other, saying, "Who is this, who even .... sins?" And He said to the woman, "Your .... has saved you; go in peace." "

DENARII	KISS
OINTMENT	MONEYLENDER
SIMON	WOMAN
FORGIVES	FAITH

THE TWO DEBTORS

Read Luke 7:40-50.
Answer the questions below.

1. To whom did Yeshua tell this parable?

....

2. How many debtors did the moneylender have?

....

3. How much money did the debtors owe the moneylender?

....

4. What did the moneylender do when the debtors could not pay?

....

5. Who did Simon say would love the moneylender more?

....

6. What did the woman do for Yeshua?

....

7. What did Simon not do for Yeshua?

....

8. "He who is _____ little, loves little."

....

9. What question did the people at the table ask each other?

....

10. What saved the woman?

....

THE TWO DEBTORS

Read Luke 7:40-50.
Find and circle each of the words from the list below.

```
Y N M O I S R N K F P R W B I W N J G T
J E L T U W Y T H C M Q D R L Q Z A U J
I U S C Z C M O N E Y L E N D E R Y U F
F S D H U O D Q S M N K Z I R T I C C R
T G L G U R K L I V G N P W A G B F V R
O G J D E A V H N L K C T B L A B O P D
G I I M O M P U S D F E A S F T E R W E
F F Z V E U N K G F V V A N U W F G P B
O A L Q K M N L N O C D O Q F Y I I J T
R B I G C Q X B M P B D Q L M S T V Q F
H E V T G M T E A R S S C Y V F X E K S
O K G I H S B U N E O L W F E N X S L S
D S A F N M Z W S Q I U F F X A Q O Z K
G H C N B S D X X I Y J N N B T I X G R
X T K M G M S E T Q M Y K K P T W G V V
M A V Y H H T Z H M K O C G O X X A G Y
D D M D J D E N A R I I N G L R O K L D
W G B C S T E V A H G E J R F J V I E R
O U U F J E R W N E Z E W O M A N A L B
C V M I A N B J G S I R N C X K T Q Q K
```

JUDGE   SINS   DEBT   MONEYLENDER
DENARII   TEARS   FORGIVES   YESHUA
WOMAN   SIMON   OIL   FAITH

www.biblepathwayadventures.com
Parables of the Messiah Activity Book
120

The Two Debtors

Draw a picture of the woman and Yeshua.

Describe a time when a friend did something nice for you.

This parable teaches me...

Imagine you are the moneylender. Would you forgive the debt of these two debtors? Why or why not?

THE TWO DEBTORS

Open your Bibles and read Luke 7:40-50.
Answer the questions. Color the picture.

1. How many denarii did the moneylender lend the two men? (verse 41)

....
....
....
....

2. What did the moneylender do when the men could not pay? (verse 42)

....
....
....
....

3. Who did Simon say would love the moneylender more? (verse 43)

....
....
....
....

 # CRACK THE CODE!

The Bible verse is written in code. Use the alphabet chart at the bottom of the page to fill in the missing letters and crack the code! *Hint: Read Luke 7:41 (ESV)*

	C	E							M			E						E				
7	22	26	19	8	7	21	1		6	13	1	26	14	24	26	1	10	26	19	18	7	10

	W		E							·			E		W	E				E
8	17	13	10	26	9	8	13	19	16		13	1	26	13	17	26	10	12	21	4	26

					E			E						,			
18	5	1	10	19	26	10		10	26	1	7	19	21	21		7	1	10

		E				E					
8	18	26	13	8	18	26	19	12	21	12	8	14

A	B	C	D	E	F	G	H	I	J	K	L	M
		22		26								6

N	O	P	Q	R	S	T	U	V	W	X	Y	Z
									17			

Let's Write

Read the parable of the Two Debtors.
Write the story in your own words on the lines below.

★ My Bible notes ★

Draw your favorite scene from this parable.

Use this space to write what God showed me today:

_____

_____

_____

_____

_____

ANSWER KEY

Parable of the Lost Sheep

What do you think? If a man has a hundred sheep and one of them has gone astray, does he not leave the ninety-nine on the mountains and go in search of the one that went astray? And if he finds it, truly, I say to you, he rejoices over it more than over the ninety-nine that never went astray. So it is not the will of My Father who is in heaven that one of these little ones should perish.

Parable of the Lost Sheep Quiz

1. The Father
2. One hundred sheep
3. On the mountains
4. He rejoices
5. In heaven
6. That no one should perish
7. Yeshua

Parable of the Lost Sheep Word Search

Parable of the Lost Sheep Coloring Activity

1. One hundred
2. One
3. He rejoiced

Parable of the Workers in the Vineyard

The kingdom of heaven is like a master of a house who hired workers for his vineyard early one morning. He agreed with the workers for a denarius a day and sent them to his vineyard. Going out about the third hour he saw others doing nothing in the marketplace and said to them, 'Go to the vineyard and whatever is right I will give you.' So they went. Going out again about the sixth hour and the ninth hour, he did the same. About the eleventh hour he went and found others standing. He said to them, 'Why do you stand here idle all day?' They said, 'Because no one has hired us.' He replied, 'You go into the vineyard too.' When evening came, the master said to his manager, 'Pay the workers their wages, beginning with the last up to the first.' When those hired at the eleventh hour came, each of them received a denarius. When those hired first came, they thought they would receive more but each of them also received a denarius. They grumbled at the master of the house, saying, 'These last worked only one hour and you have made them equal to us who have worked all day in the heat.' He replied to one of them, 'Friend, I am being fair with you. You agreed to work for a denarius. Take what belongs to you and go. I choose to give to this last worker the same as you. Am I not allowed to do what I choose with what belongs to me? Or do you begrudge my generosity?' So the last will be first and the first last.

Parable of the Workers in the Vineyard Quiz

1. A master of a vineyard
2. Early morning
3. One denarius
4. Into his vineyard
5. Four times
6. The foreman (manager)
7. Beginning with the last up to the first
8. Because they thought they would be paid more than the workers who had worked less hours
9. Friend, I am doing you no wrong. Did you not agree with me for a denarius? Take what belongs to you and go. I choose to give to this last worker as I give to you. Am I not allowed to do what I choose with what belongs to me? Or do you begrudge my generosity?
10. First

Parable of the Workers in the Vineyard Word Search

Parable of the Workers in the Vineyard Coloring Activity
1. A denarius a day
2. The foreman (manager)
3. First

Parable of the Mustard Seed
He said, "With what can we compare the kingdom of God, or what parable shall we use for it? It is like a grain of mustard seed, which when sown on the ground is the smallest of all the seeds on earth. Yet when it is sown, it grows up and becomes larger than all the garden plants and puts out large branches, so that the birds of the air can make nests in its shade."
With many such parables He spoke the word to them, as they were able to hear it. He did not speak to them without a parable. But privately to His own disciples, Yeshua explained everything.

Parable of the Mustard Seed Quiz
1. Like a grain of mustard seed
2. Smallest of all the seeds
3. Larger than all the garden plants
4. Make nests in its branches
5. Parables
6. He explained everything to His disciples
7. Yeshua

Parable of the Mustard Seed Word Search

A Disciple Coloring Activity
1. Twelve
2. He used parables to explain his ideas
3. He explained His teachings to them

Parable of the Good Samaritan
The Torah teacher, desiring to justify himself said to Yeshua, "Who is my neighbor?" Yeshua replied, "A man was going down from Jerusalem to Jericho and fell among robbers, who stripped him, beat him and departed, leaving him half dead. Now by chance a priest was going down that road, and when he saw him he passed by on the other side. Likewise, a Levite when he came to the place and saw him, passed by on the other side. But a Samaritan, as he journeyed, came to where he was and when he saw him, he had compassion. He bound up his wounds, pouring on oil and wine. Then he set him on his own animal and brought him to an inn and took care of him. The next day he took out two denarii and gave them to the innkeeper, saying, 'Take care of him, and whatever more you spend I will repay you when I come back.' Which of these three do you think proved to be a neighbor to the man who fell among the robbers?" He said, "The one who showed him mercy." And Yeshua said to him, "Go and do likewise."

Parable of the Good Samaritan Quiz

1. A Torah teacher (lawyer)
2. "You shall love God with all your heart, soul, and strength; and your neighbor as yourself." (Deuteronomy 6:5)
3. To Jericho
4. He was robbed and beaten
5. A priest
6. A Levite
7. A Samaritan
8. Cleaned his wounds and paid an innkeeper to take care of him
9. Two denarii
10. "He who showed mercy on him."

Parable of the Good Samaritan Word Search

The Good Samaritan Coloring Activity

1. A Samaritan
2. Two denarii
3. The man who showed him mercy

Parable of the Wise and Foolish Virgins

The kingdom of heaven will be like ten virgins who took their lamps and went to meet the bridegroom. Five of them were foolish and five were wise. When the foolish took their lamps, they took no oil with them. But the wise took flasks of oil with their lamps. As the bridegroom was delayed, they all became drowsy and slept. But at midnight there was a cry, 'Here is the bridegroom! Come out to meet Him.' Then all the virgins rose and trimmed their lamps. The foolish virgins said to the wise, 'Give us some of your oil for our lamps are going out.' But the wise virgins said, 'Since there will not be enough for us and for you, go to the dealers and buy for yourselves.' And while

they were going to buy, the bridegroom came and those who were ready went in with Him to the marriage feast and the door was shut. Afterward the other virgins came, saying, 'Lord, open to us.' But He answered, 'Truly, I say to you, I do not know you.' Watch therefore, for you know neither the day nor the hour.

Parable of the Wise and Foolish Virgins Quiz

1. Ten
2. Five
3. The virgins all slept
4. Midnight
5. Go out to meet the bridegroom
6. Lamps with no oil
7. Lamps full of oil
8. Give us some of your oil for our lamps are going out
9. The bridegroom arrived and went into the wedding with the wise virgins, and shut the door
10. He said He did not know them

Parable of the Wise and Foolish Virgins Word Search

Parable of the Wise and Foolish Virgins Coloring Activity

1. Ten
2. Five
3. The virgins who were ready (the five virgins with oil)

Parable of the Wedding Feast

The kingdom of heaven is compared to a king who gave a wedding feast for his son and sent servants to call those who were invited to the feast, but they would not come. Again he sent more servants, saying, 'Tell those who are invited, "I have prepared my dinner, my oxen and calves have been killed and everything is ready. Come to the feast."' But they paid no

attention and went off, one to his farm, one to his business, while the rest seized his servants, treated them badly and killed them. The king was angry. He sent his troops and destroyed the murderers and burned their city. Then he said to his servants, 'The wedding feast is ready but those invited were not worthy. Go and invite as many as you find.' The servants went and gathered all whom they found, both bad and good. The wedding hall was filled with guests. But when the king came in to look at the guests, he saw a man who had no wedding garment. He said to him, 'Friend, how did you get in here without a wedding garment?' And he was speechless. The king said to the attendants, 'Bind him hand and foot and cast him into outer darkness. In that place there will be weeping and gnashing of teeth.' Many are called but few are chosen.

Parable of the Wedding Feast Quiz
1. Yeshua
2. A king who gave a wedding feast for his son
3. The king's son
4. Oxen and fat calves
5. They were treated shamefully and killed
6. The king was angry that people had killed his servants
7. From the main roads
8. A man not wearing a wedding garment
9. Bind him hand and foot and cast him into the outer darkness
10. Called

Parable of the Wedding Feast Word Search

Parable of the Wedding Feast Coloring Activity
1. His servants
2. They were treated shamefully and killed
3. The roads

Parable of the Prodigal Son
A man had two sons. The younger son said to his father, 'Give me my share of the inheritance.' The man divided his wealth between them. A few days later, the younger son gathered all he had, went to a far land and wasted his inheritance on foolish living. When he had spent everything, there was a famine and he became hungry. He got a job with a man who sent him into his fields to feed pigs. He was so hungry that he wanted the food that the pigs ate. But no one gave him anything. He said, 'My father's hired workers have plenty of food. I have nothing to eat. I will return home and say to my father, "I have sinned against heaven and before you. I am no longer worthy to be called your son. Treat me as one of your hired workers."' He left and went to his father. While he was still a long way off, his father saw him coming. He felt compassion and ran to him, and hugged and kissed him. The son said, 'I have sinned against heaven and before you. I am not worthy to be called your son.' The father said to his workers, 'Put the best robe on him, put a ring on his hand and shoes on his feet. Kill the best calf and let us eat and celebrate. My son was dead, and is alive again; he was lost and now is found.' So they began to celebrate. The older son was in the field and as he came near the house, he heard music and dancing. He asked a servant what was happening. He said, 'You father has killed the best calf because your brother is back home safely.' But the son was angry and refused to go in. His father came out and pleaded with him, but he said, 'I have served you for many years and never disobeyed you. You never gave me a young goat to celebrate with my friends. But my brother comes home who has used his inheritance with prostitutes and you killed the best calf for him!' He said to him, 'Son, you are always with me and everything I have is yours. It was fitting to celebrate and be happy - your brother was dead and is alive; he was lost and is found.'

Parable of the Prodigal Son Quiz
1. Two sons
2. Youngest son
3. A far away country
4. There was a famine
5. Feeding pigs
6. He came to his senses (repentance)
7. The eldest son
8. Ran to his son, threw his arms around him and kissed him
9. Good shoes, clothes and a ring
10. Killed a fatted calf and had a party

Parable of the Prodigal Son Word Search

The Prodigal Son Coloring Activity

1. Gave him the best clothes, a ring, and sandals to wear, and killed a fatted calf
2. Because his son was back home safely
3. He had always obeyed his father, but his father had never given him the same type of celebration. And he thought his brother had wasted his money on foolish living

Parable of the Talents

It will be like a man going on a journey who entrusted his servants with his property. To one he gave five talents, to another two, to another one, each according to his ability. Then he went away. He who had received five talents went at once and traded with them, and made five talents more. He who had two talents made two talents more. But he who had received one talent dug in the ground and hid his master's money. After a long time, their master came and settled accounts with them. He who received five talents came forward, bringing five talents more, saying, 'Master, you delivered to me five talents; here, I have made five talents more.' His master said to him, 'Well done, good and faithful servant. You have been faithful over a little; I will set you over much. Enter into the joy of your master.' He who had two talents came forward, saying, 'Master, you delivered to me two talents; here, I have made two talents more.' His master said to him, 'Well done, good and faithful servant. You have been faithful over a little; I will set you over much. Enter into the joy of your master.' He who had received the one talent came forward, saying, 'Master, I knew you to be a hard man, reaping where you did not sow, and gathering where you scattered no seed, so I was afraid and hid your talent in the ground. Here, you have what is yours.' His master said, 'You wicked and slothful servant! You knew that I reap where I have not sown and gather where I scattered no seed? You should have invested my money with

the bankers and at my coming I should have received what was mine with interest. Take the talent from him and give it to him who has ten talents. For everyone who has will more be given, and he will have an abundance. But from the one who has not, even what he has will be taken away. Cast the worthless servant into the outer darkness where there will be weeping and gnashing of teeth.'

Parable of the Talents Quiz

1. Five talents
2. Two talents
3. One talent
4. Traded with them and made five more talents
5. Gained two more talents
6. Dug a hole in the ground and buried his talent
7. Well done, good and faithful servants, you have been faithful over a little; I will put you in charge of much.
8. I was afraid and hid your talent in the ground
9. He became angry
10. Took the talent and gave it to the servant who had ten talents

Parable of the Talents Word Search

Parable of the Talents Coloring Activity

1. He traded them and made five more talents
2. He was afraid
3. Outer darkness

Parable of the Rich Man and Lazarus

There was a rich man clothed in purple and fine linen, who feasted every day. At his gate lay a poor man named Lazarus, covered with sores, who desired to be fed with food that fell from the rich man's table. Even the dogs came and licked his sores. The poor man died and was carried by the angels to

Abraham's side. The rich man also died and was buried. In Hades, being in torment, he lifted up his eyes and saw Abraham far off and Lazarus at his side. He called out, 'Father Abraham, have mercy on me and send Lazarus to dip the end of his finger in water and cool my tongue, for I am in anguish in this flame.' But Abraham said, 'Child, remember that in your lifetime you received your good things. And Lazarus received bad things; but now he is comforted here and you are in anguish. A great chasm has been fixed between you and us so that those who would pass from here to you may not be able, and none may cross from there to us.' And he said, 'I beg you to send him to my father's house— for I have five brothers—so that he can warn them in case they also come into this place.' But Abraham said, 'They have Moses and the Prophets; let them hear them.' And he said, 'No, father Abraham, if someone goes to them from the dead, they will repent.' He said to him, 'If they do not hear Moses and the Prophets, neither will they be convinced if someone should rise from the dead.'

Parable of the Rich Man and Lazarus Quiz

1. Purple and fine linen
2. A man named Lazarus
3. The angels carried him to Abraham's side
4. Hades (or Sheol)
5. Abraham
6. Send Lazarus to dip the end of his finger in water and cool my tongue
7. To his father's house
8. Five brothers
9. Moses
10. Because they would have seen Lazarus raised from the dead

Parable of the Rich Man and Lazarus Word Search

Rich Man and Lazarus Coloring Activity

1. Abraham and Lazarus
2. To send Lazarus to dip his finger in water and cool his tongue
3. To warn them about this place of torment

Parable of the Sower

Again Yeshua began to teach beside the sea. A large crowd gathered around Him, so He got into a boat and sat in it on the sea, and the whole crowd was beside the sea on the land. And He was teaching them many things in parables. In His teaching, He said to them: "Listen! Behold, a sower went out to sow. And as he sowed, some seed fell along the path and the birds came and ate it. Other seed fell on rocky ground where it did not have much soil, and immediately it sprang up since it had no depth of soil. And when the sun rose, it was scorched and since it had no root, it withered away. Other seed fell among thorns, and the thorns grew up and choked it and it grew no grain. And other seeds fell into good soil and produced grain, growing up and increasing and yielding thirtyfold and sixtyfold and a hundredfold." Yeshua said, "He who has ears to hear, let him hear."

Parable of the Sower Quiz

1. Yeshua
2. In a boat
3. Beside the sea
4. The birds ate the seed
5. When the sun rose, it was scorched and withered away
6. The thorns grew up and choked the seed, and no grain grew
7. The seeds produced grain, growing up and increasing and yielding thirtyfold and sixtyfold and a hundredfold
8. To you has been given the secret of the kingdom of God, but for those outside everything is in parables, so that they may see but not perceive and may hear but not understand, lest they should turn and be forgiven
9. The Word that has been sown along the path
10. They produce good fruit, thirtyfold and sixtyfold and a hundredfold

Parable of the Sower Word Search

The Sower Coloring Activity

1. By the sea
2. The thorns grew up and choked the seed and it produced no grain
3. The seed produced grain, growing up and increasing and yielding thirtyfold, sixtyfold and a hundredfold

Parable of the Wise and Foolish Builders

Everyone then who hears these words of Mine and does them will be like a wise man who built his house on the rock. The rain fell and the floods came, the winds blew and beat on that house, but it did not fall because it had been founded on the rock. Everyone who hears these words of Mine and does not do them will be like a foolish man who built his house on the sand. And the rain fell and the floods came, and the winds blew and beat against that house, and it fell and great was the fall of it.

Parable of the Wise and Foolish Builders Quiz

1. Yeshua
2. A wise man
3. The house was built on the rock
4. Foolish
5. Sand
6. It fell to the ground

Parable of the Wise and Foolish Builders Word Search

Wise and Foolish Builders Coloring Activity

1. The wise man listened to Yeshua and build his house on the rock
2. He did not listen to Yeshua and do what He said
3. His house fell to the ground

Parable of the Rich Fool

Yeshua told them a parable, saying, "The land of a rich man produced many crops and he thought to himself, 'What shall I do - I have nowhere to store my crops?' And he said, 'I will do this: I will tear down my barns and build larger ones, and there I will store all my grain and goods. And I will say to my soul, "Soul, you have many goods laid up for many years; relax, eat, drink, be merry."' But Yahweh said to him, 'Fool! This night your soul is required of you and the things you have prepared, whose will they be?' So is the one who lays up treasure for himself and is not rich toward God."

Parable of the Rich Fool Quiz

1. Yeshua
2. Many crops
3. Tear down his barns and build larger ones
4. Relax eat drink and be merry
5. "Fool! This night your soul is required of you and the things you have prepared, whose will they be?"
6. So is the person who lays up treasure for himself and is not rich toward God

Parable of the Rich Fool Word Search

The Rich Fool Coloring Activity
1. He had nowhere to store his crops
2. All his grain and goods
3. "Fool! This night your soul is required of you and the things you have prepared, whose will they be?"

Parable of the Pharisee and the Tax Collector
Yeshua told this parable to some people who thought they were righteous and treated others with contempt: "Two men went up into the temple to pray, one a Pharisee and the other a tax collector. The Pharisee, standing alone, prayed, 'God, thank you that I am not like other men who cheat, are unjust, adulterers, or even like this tax collector. I fast twice a week; I give tithes of all that I get.' But the tax collector, standing far off, would not even lift up his eyes to heaven, but beat his breast, saying, 'God, have mercy on me. I am a sinner!' I tell you, this man went down to his house justified rather than the Pharisee. For everyone who exalts himself will be humbled, but the one who humbles himself will be exalted.

Parable of the Pharisee and the Tax Collector Quiz
1. Yeshua
2. A Pharisee and a tax collector
3. To pray
4. Two times a week
5. Upwards (to heaven)
6. "God, be merciful to me, a sinner!"
7. Justified
8. Humbled

Parable of the Pharisee and the Tax Collector Word Search

The Pharisee Coloring Activity
1. Some who thought they were righteous, and treated others with contempt
2. A Pharisee and a tax collector
3. Because he fasted twice a week and tithed

Parable of the Faithful Servant
Peter said, "Yeshua, are you telling this parable for us or for all people?" Yeshua said, "Who then is the faithful and wise manager whom his master will set over his household to give them their portion of food at the proper time? Blessed is that servant whom his master will find doing so when he comes. Truly, I say to you, he will set him over all his possessions. But if that servant says to himself, 'My master is delayed in coming,' and begins to beat other servants, and to eat and drink and get drunk, the master of that servant will come on a day when the servant is not ready and not expecting him, and will cut him in pieces and put him with the unfaithful. That servant who knew his master's will but did not get ready or do what the master wanted, will receive a severe beating. But the one who did not know, and did what deserved a beating, will receive a light beating. To whoever much was given, much will be required. And much more will be expected from the one who has been given more.

Parable of the Faithful Servant Quiz
1. Yeshua
2. Peter
3. A faithful and wise manager
4. The servant who does what the master has asked him to do
5. He will be given responsibility for all the master's possessions

6. When the master returns, he will cut him in pieces and put him with the unfaithful
7. The servant who knew his master's will be did not get ready and do this
8. He will receive a light beating
9. Much

Parable of the Faithful Servant Word Search

The Faithful Servant Coloring Activity
1. To take care of his master's household
2. The master will set him over all his possessions
3. Given

Parable of the Two Debtors

Yeshua said to Simon, "I have something to say to you." And he answered, "Say it, Teacher." "A certain moneylender had two debtors. One owed 500 denarii, and the other 50 denarii. When they could not pay, he cancelled the debt of both. Which of them will love him more?" Simon answered, "The one, I suppose, for whom he cancelled the larger debt." Yeshua said to him, "You have judged rightly." Then He turned toward the woman and said to Simon, "Do you see this woman? I entered your house; you gave Me no water for My feet, but she has wet My feet with her tears and wiped them with her hair. You gave Me no kiss, but from the time I came in she has not ceased to kiss My feet. You did not anoint My head with oil, but she has anointed My feet with ointment. I tell you, her many sins are forgiven—for she loved much. But he who is forgiven little, loves little." And He said to her, "Your sins are forgiven." Then those who were at table with Him began talking to each other, saying, "Who is this, who even forgives sins?" And He said to the woman, "Your faith has saved you; go in peace."

Parable of the Two Debtors Quiz
1. Simon
2. Two debtors
3. One owed 500 denarii and the other owed 50 denarii
4. Cancelled their debts
5. The person with the larger debt
6. Wet His feet, dried them with her hair, kissed His feet, and anointed them with ointment
7. Gave Him no water for his feet, no kiss, and did not anoint His head with oil
8. Forgiven
9. Who is this man who forgives sins?
10. Her faith

Parable of the Two Debtors Word Search

The Two Debtors Coloring Activity

1. He gave one 500 denarii, and the other 50 denarii
2. He cancelled their debts
3. The debtor with the bigger debt

◆◇ DISCOVER MORE ACTIVITY BOOKS! ◇◆

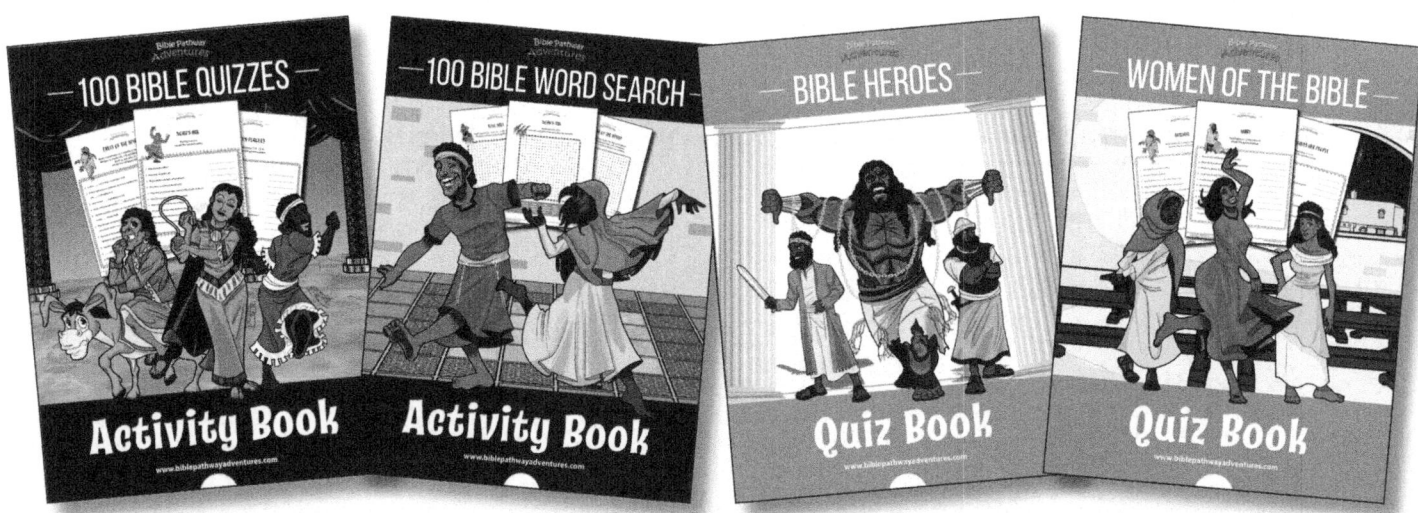

Available for purchase at www.biblepathwayadventures.com

Made in the USA
Las Vegas, NV
16 November 2021